Philip Croucher

MacIntyre Purcell Publishing Inc.

Copyright © 2019 Philip Croucher

All rights reserved. No part of this book covered by the copyrights hereon may be reproduced or used in any form or by any means – graphic, electronic, or mechanical – without the prior written permission of the publisher. Any request for photocopying, recording, taping, or information storage and retrieval systems of any part of this book shall be directed in writing to the Canadian Reprography Collective, 379 Adelaide Street, West, Suite M1, Toronto, Ontario, M5V 1S5.

MacIntyre Purcell Publishing Inc.
194 Hospital Rd.
Lunenburg, Nova Scotia
B0J 2C0

(902) 640-3350
www.macintyrepurcell.com
info@macintyrepurcell.com

Printed and bound in Canada by Friesens

Book design: Denis Cunningham
Cover design: Denis Cunningham

Cover photo credits:
Sidney Crosby (Josh Holmberg/Hockey Hall of Fame)
Nathan MacKinnon (Rusty Barton/Hockey Hall of Fame)
Brad Marchand (Rusty Barton/Hockey Hall of Fame)

ISBN: 978-1-77276-139-9

Library and Archives Canada Cataloguing in Publication

Title: The three stars / Philip Croucher.
Names: Croucher, Philip, author.
Identifiers: Canadiana 20190127945 | ISBN 9781772761399 (softcover)
Subjects: LCSH: Hockey players—Nova Scotia—Biography. | LCSH: National Hockey League—Biography. |
LCSH: Crosby, Sidney, 1987- | LCSH: MacKinnon, Nathan, 1995- | LCSH: Marchand, Brad, 1988-
Classification: LCC GV848.5.A1 C76 2019 | DDC 796.962092/2—dc23

MacIntyre Purcell Publishing Inc. would like to acknowledge the financial support of the Government of Canada and the Nova Scotia Department of Tourism, Culture and Heritage.

Funded by the Government of Canada | Canadä   NOVA SCOTIA

"The biggest thing for me is the passion that I've always had for hockey. I can say going through different things that that passion is the most important part. It's not skills or talent or any of that stuff."

— Sidney Crosby

TABLE OF CONTENTS

Foreword 6

Author Note 10

Introduction: Crosby, Marchand and MacKinnon 13

Chapter 1: Our Hockey History 21

Chapter 2: The Sidney Crosby Story:
From Phenom to Superstar 31

Chapter 3: Sidney Crosby's Season:
By the Numbers 43

Chapter 4: The Brad Marchand Story:
Bulldog Makes it as a Bruin 55

Chapter 5: Brad Marchand's Season: By the Numbers 69

Chapter 6: The Nathan MacKinnon Story:
The Next 'Next One'? 81

Chapter 7: Nathan MacKinnon's Season:
By the Numbers 95

Chapter 8: Training Together 107

Chapter 9: Giving Back 117

Chapter 10: The Legacy 125

FOREWORD

I often give a lot of thought to the subject of what is the best Canadian hockey province. By that I mean of course, the province that produces the greatest number of talented players.

Obviously, it's not Nova Scotia.

It would be historically inaccurate to say otherwise.

Gretzky, Orr, Lemieux, Howe, Hull, Lafleur, Richard, Beliveau, Coffey, Messier, McDavid. They all come from provinces not called Nova Scotia. Those truths can't be argued.

But from a contemporary point of view, the performance of three current NHL players raises some interesting questions about where Nova Scotia should rank. If we were to hold a draft today and select only forwards, would Sidney Crosby, Nathan MacKinnon and Brad Marchand be on everyone's Top 5 list?

Top 10 list maybe?

Likely.

They'd be on mine.

Let's put it this way: Nova Scotia has come a long way. I recall two decades earlier, the pride I felt watching Glen Murray and Al MacInnis play in the NHL. They were my two favourite players solely based on two criteria: how they played and where they grew up. I followed them and cheered them on in a very special way, feeling pure Nova Scotia provincial pride as I witnessed their on-ice success from afar.

But what we have happening in today's NHL has taken things to an unimaginable level. Crosby, MacKinnon and Marchand are dominating the NHL and it appears they're actually getting better, not worse with the passage of time. It's staggering. And it's not gone unnoticed by the hockey community at large.

This little gem of a province that we call home - a peninsula in the North Atlantic with a population fewer than a million - has produced three incredibly successful NHL stars.

I've never seen the proverbial 'hockey map', but if one exists, Crosby, MacKinnon and Marchand have put Nova Scotia on it.

The book you hold in your hands celebrates these three stars. Philip Croucher always gets it right and on this subject he's tapped into a true NHL conversation piece: our three Nova Scotia stars are killing it.

Enjoy the book and enjoy the upcoming season. Sid, Nathan and Brad are a treat to watch.

Paul Hollingsworth is a correspondent for TSN and also works for CTV Atlantic. He lives in Dartmouth and has been covering sports for decades. He is the author of several books, including Sidney Crosby: The Story of a Champion *and* Nathan MacKinnon: The NHL's Rising Star.

(Clockwise from top) Brad Marchand (Paul Stinsa/Hockey Hall of Fame)
Nathan MacKinnon (Rusty Barton/Hockey Hall of Fame)
Sidney Crosby (Josh Holmberg/Hockey Hall of Fame)

AUTHOR NOTE

It was an incredible year for Nova Scotia hockey and to be able to tell the stories of Sidney Crosby, Brad Marchand and Nathan MacKinnon through their amazing seasons is truly humbling.

All three are special talents and this book serves as a keepsake for their accomplishments as a trio. It was historic and will be talked about for generations.

A special thank you to all who helped make this project a reality, including everyone at MacIntyre Purcell Publishing Inc. for trusting me with telling an important story in our province's rich sports history.

To Paul Hollingsworth, thank you for delivering the perfect foreword and for putting into perspective about how great these players are in today's NHL.

To Ken Reid, Brad Crossley, Darren Cossar, John Moore, Trey Lewis, Matthew Stienburg and Trevor Stienburg, thank you for providing amazing insights into the special season that we witnessed and its lasting impact. The book wouldn't have been possible without you.

I'm proud of the work that went into *The Three Stars* and I hope everyone enjoys reading it. We are lucky to call Crosby, MacKinnon and Marchand our own. They serve as great inspiration for people and remind us that anything is possible through hard work and perseverance.

Philip Croucher

DEDICATION

To my family for their continued support and to hockey fans across this great province and country.

Also, to Sidney, Brad and Nathan for being superstars both on and off the ice.

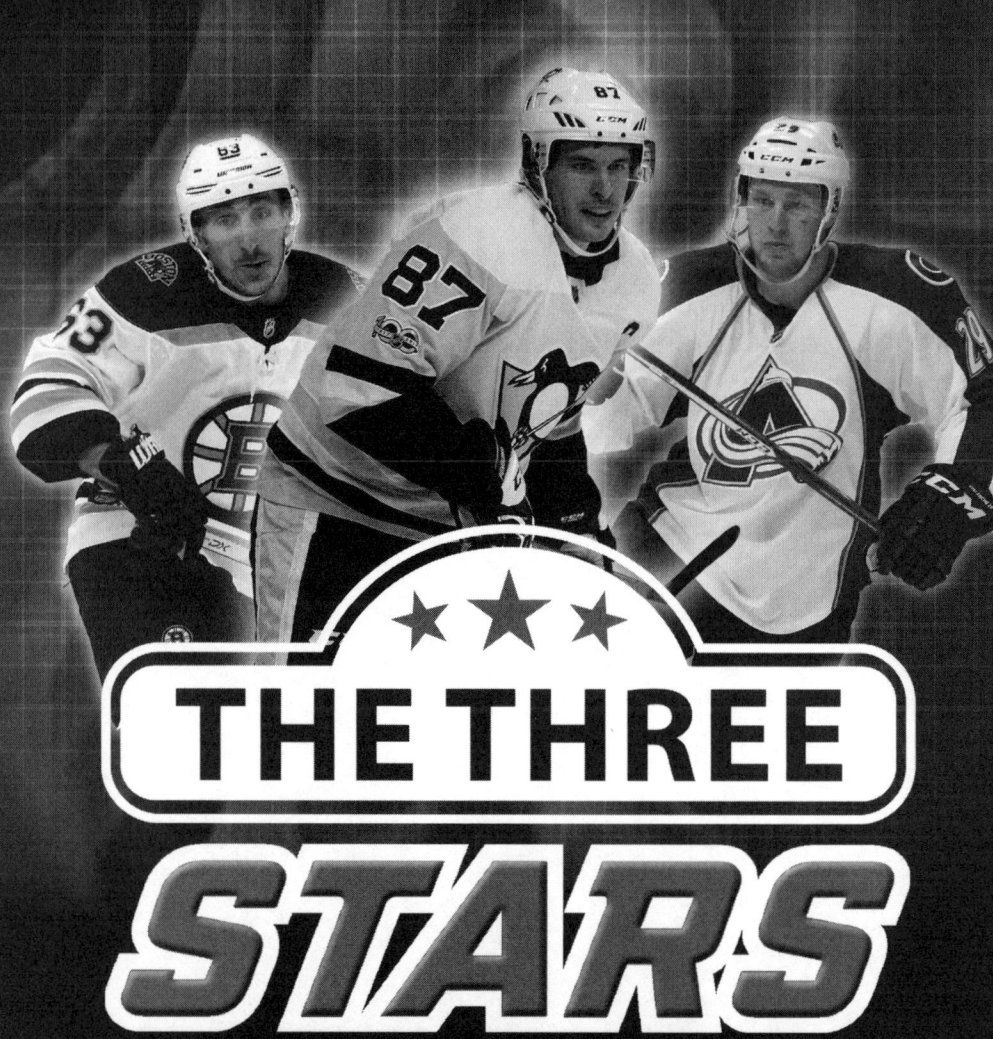

INTRODUCTION
CROSBY, MARCHAND and MACKINNON

They step onto the ice together each summer as friends. As hockey players are hard-wired to do, there's banter, stick-jabs – even a few love-taps. But when the on-ice training officially begins during off-season practices at the BMO Centre in Bedford, Nova Scotia, the funny business ends, and the work begins for hockey superstars Sidney Crosby, Nathan MacKinnon and Brad Marchand.

If you're lucky enough to be sharing the ice with them, good luck keeping up.

"When the puck drops they go at it hard. It's like a switch," says Brad Crossley, an elite hockey trainer who runs summer practices for professional players from the Halifax region.

"In between drills, or in the dressing room, they're friends. In practice when they're on the ice, it's intense, it's in your face. They chirp one another and don't back down. They bring an intensity that is unheard of."

You know something else that is unheard of? Nova Scotia having three hockey players as good as Crosby, MacKinnon and Marchand at one time. All three are from Halifax Regional Municipality. Crosby and MacKinnon grew up in Cole Harbour, and Marchand is from Hammonds Plains.

Just how good were Crosby, MacKinnon and Marchand last season in the NHL? They combined for a whopping 299 points and each finished in the Top 10 for overall scoring. Crosby and Marchand recorded 100 points apiece – the unofficial mark of a big season offensively. MacKinnon ended with 99 but was the only one of the three to score more than 40 goals.

The impressiveness doesn't end there. Crosby, MacKinnon and Marchand each finished in the top six in NHL MVP voting. Crosby was runner-up to Tampa Bay Lightning forward Nikita Kucherov and placed ahead of Edmonton Oilers superstar Connor McDavid. Marchand was fifth behind Calgary Flames sniper Johnny Gaudreau, with MacKinnon coming in at No. 6 ahead of Washington Capitals sniper Alex Ovechkin.

Put this all together and the argument could be made that Halifax and Nova Scotia have the cream of the crop in Canada, even the world, for the biggest marquee superstars in the game today.

"It's almost now, in a way, you take it for granted because they're such good players," says Sportsnet anchor and Nova Scotian Ken Reid. "I wasn't shocked to see them all come in around 100 points. It's really special, but I almost think we take it for granted because these three have been so good for so long."

That's why the title for this book, *The Three Stars*, fits so nicely. They're not only three stars in the NHL and the hockey world, but they're our three stars. We're lucky to call them our own.

The book explores our rich hockey history in Nova Scotia and how Crosby, MacKinnon and Marchand have changed the way fans and NHL executives look at players we produce. The book also examines how each of the three made it to the NHL, and it breaks down their remarkable 2018-19 seasons individually.

We also look at the impact of these great players both on and off the ice in Nova Scotia. The future looks bright. Maybe not bright enough to match last season's remarkable feat, but who knows? "I never thought you would have a year with three Nova Scotians in the Top 10 in scoring," says Darren Cossar, the former executive director for Hockey Nova Scotia, who is now working with Hockey Canada.

"I believe with what they've done, they keep setting the bar higher for Nova Scotian athletes, and for the next group that comes along."

NHL SCORING LEADERS 2018-19

		G	A	P
1	Nikita Kucherov, Tampa Bay	41	87	128
2	Connor McDavid, Edmonton	41	75	116
3	Patrick Kane, Chicago	44	66	110
4	Leon Draisaitl, Edmonton	50	55	105
5	Brad Marchand, Boston	36	64	100
6	Sidney Crosby, Pittsburgh	35	65	100
7	Nathan MacKinnon, Colorado	41	58	99
8	Johnny Gaudreau, Calgary	36	63	99
9	Steven Stamkos, Tampa Bay	45	53	98
10	Aleksander Barkov, Florida	31	65	96

Source: NHL.com

NHL MVP VOTING 2019

1	Nikita Kucherov, Tampa Bay	1677
2	Sidney Crosby, Pittsburgh	739
3	Connor McDavid, Edmonton	465
4	Johnny Gaudreau, Calgary	442
5	Brad Marchand, Boston	322
6	Nathan MacKinnon, Colorado	265
7	Alex Ovechkin, Washington	213
8	Patrick Kane, Chicago	125
9	Mark Giordano, Calgary	66
10	Sebastien Aho, Carolina	21
11	Jordan Binnington, St. Louis	21

Source: Professional Hockey Writers Association

"Hockey's place in Canadian culture is closer to religion than a simple sporting pastime, a unifying force in a country of 33 million people that is often split by politics and language."

-- Steve Keating, Reuters

"Sidney Crosby is a great ambassador for hockey all over the world, and I think Nathan MacKinnon is becoming that. And Brad Marchand is ... a guy that really matured and his teammates love him. And I love hearing that about him."

— former Nova Scotia NHLer Jody Shelley

(Previous pages) Hockey in Nova Scotia has come a long way, thanks in large part to the success of its current superstars Sidney Crosby, Brad Marchand and Nathan MacKinnon. NHL scouts are discovering more top players from the province.

CHAPTER 1
OUR HOCKEY HISTORY

Ken Reid gets to watch and talk hockey for a living.

Born and raised in Pictou, Nova Scotia, Reid moved to Halifax after high school and began broadcasting junior A games for the now-defunct Dartmouth Oland Exports. In 1996, he left the province to work in TV broadcasting in Calgary, Ottawa and then Edmonton. He moved to Toronto in 2008 and three years later began working at Sportsnet where he remains today, as co-anchor of the popular Sportsnet Central prime-time weeknight show with Evanka Osmak.

Reid is a proud Nova Scotian and loves to name-drop the hometowns of hockey players when he's on the air. That means if you score a goal or make a big save on a Sportsnet highlight reel package, Reid will undoubtedly make sure his audience knows where you're from.

"When Joey MacDonald was playing in the NHL, I'd say Pictou, Nova Scotia. ... Same for Colin White, Derrick Walser," he says in an interview.

"When Sid does something, he's from Cole Harbour. When Nathan does something, he's from Cole Harbour. If Brad does something, he's from Hammonds Plains. And when the (Halifax) Mooseheads were hosting the Memorial Cup this year, and they were doing well, I'd make sure to say they were going wild at the Midtown Tavern."

Reid is a student of the game and loves to talk about Nova Scotia hockey. Growing up, his hockey heroes from the province were Winnipeg Jets sniper Paul MacLean of Antigonish and Montreal Canadians forward Mike McPhee of River Bourgeois. Before the 2018-19 season, only four Nova Scotia players had surpassed 100 points in a season. MacLean was one of them.

Crosby did it a remarkable five times before last season, but not since the 2013-14 campaign when he finished with 104 points.

Hall of Fame defenceman Al MacInnis of Port Hood reached 103 points during the 1990-91 season with the Calgary Flames.

MacLean recorded his 100-point campaign during the 1984-85 season, with 41 goals and 101 points playing on a line with star centre Dale Hawerchuk.

Bobby Smith, who was born in North Sydney but moved to Ottawa at an early age, also reached the 100-point mark with the Minnesota North Stars during the 1981-82 season, notching 114 points.

HISTORIC, INCREDIBLE TALENT

This history shows how remarkable last season was for Nova Scotia hockey. Sidney Crosby and Brad Marchand reaching 100 points marked the first time two players from Nova Scotia accomplished the feat in the same season. MacKinnon, of course, fell just one point short of making it three.

"When you think they're from a province of one million – that's pretty incredible," Reid says. "Then when you shrink it down a little more, and two of them are from Cole Harbour, and one is from Hammonds Plains, that makes it even more special.

Pittsburgh Penguins captain Sidney Crosby waves to the crowd during a Stanley Cup parade in his hometown of Cole Harbour, Nova Scotia on Friday, August 7, 2009. The event coincided with Crosby's 22nd birthday.

"This is easily the most talented group of Nova Scotians we have ever had in the NHL at one point. That is no disrespect to the people that came before, like Al MacInnis. When Al MacInnis was doing his thing, there was only one Al MacInnis. It wasn't like there were three of Al. Now, there are three all around 100 points. That's pretty incredible."

Trevor Stienburg echoes the sentiment. Born and raised in Kingston, Ontario, Stienburg has been calling Halifax his home for more than two decades after a 10-year professional career that saw him play 71 games for the NHL's Quebec Nordiques. He also played parts of two seasons for the Halifax Citadels of the American Hockey League between 1989 and 1991.

Stienburg is the longtime coach of the Saint Mary's Huskies men's hockey team and knows how special last season was for hockey in Nova Scotia and the East Coast in general.

"I think everybody in the Maritimes, certainly in the Halifax area, could not be prouder or feel better about three guys in the Top 10 in the NHL for scoring who basically live within the city limits," he says. "That's incredibly special.

"I think all three are exceptional guys too. I am a big fan of Brad. He does so many things and doesn't care if people know it."

According to the Hockey Hall of Fame, only 72 players born in Nova Scotia played in the NHL before the 2019-20 season. You can throw in a handful of others too, like Yarmouth's Jody Shelley and MacLean, both of whom moved to the province at an early age.

Making the NHL from Nova Scotia remains a tough grind. It was even harder for players before the mid-1990s and the beginning of the Quebec Major Junior Hockey League's Maritime expansion.

Players back in those days didn't have elite teams to suit up for close to home and NHL teams didn't have the technology or ability to watch games and see highlights from faraway players like they do today.

GRINDERS TO DIAMONDS

The result was countless players from Nova Scotia had to pack their bags, leave their families for long distances, and see if they could make it.

Sure-fire NHLers like Crosby and MacKinnon simply didn't exist back then.

"I remember growing up thinking if you're from Nova Scotia and you're going to make it, you have to be a grinder," Reid said. "Then all of a sudden you hear about this kid Sidney Crosby and then Nathan comes along and Brad comes along, and you don't have to be a grinder anymore to make it from Nova Scotia."

Darren Cossar, vice-president of member engagement at Hockey Canada, agrees with Reid's assessment about how Nova Scotia players needed grit and determination to get noticed pre-2000. But he also thinks those built-in traits are helping the more skilled players the province is producing.

"Some of those grinders, those tough guys, take no guck, do the extra things in the corners, working hard and battling for pucks, trying to prove themselves at that level – by them breaking through and those players becoming those regular third and fourth liners – it put hockey in the mind of 'we can make it,'" Cossar says. "The next set of kids, we're going to have all that grit and determination, but we are also going to have that skill."

Cossar believes the turning point for hockey in Nova Scotia came in the 2000s. He refers to that time period as "the perfect storm."

Crosby was a huge factor, he says: knowing a talent like his from Nova Scotia could go No. 1 in the NHL draft and draw comparisons to Wayne Gretzky, arguably the greatest hockey player ever.

"Sidney is just an absolute special individual. It was like, 'Holy smokes, someone from here can be that good?'"

But a long line of events made Halifax a hockey hotspot too: the 2003 World Junior Hockey Championships, the 2004 World Women's Hockey Championship, followed in 2008 with the World Men's Hockey Championship.

"Then prior to that, the Mooseheads and the Quebec league coming. You just add one plus one plus one plus one, it adds up," Cossar says.

"All of those things put hockey front and centre for all the positive reasons. It showed a real connection where we don't have an NHL team and kids can connect to and really identify with. All of a sudden, the top players in the world were here and kids could see that up front. It made it seem more real to kids and pushed that drive and built that determination."

The impact of the Quebec Major Junior Hockey League expansion into the Maritimes on player development for Canada's East Coast can't be overstated. Kids idolize these players, and they can really reach that level. It stares them in the face every time they go to games in Halifax, Sydney, Charlottetown, Moncton, Saint John or Bathurst.

The rosters for the 18 QMJHL teams show an influx of East Coast talent, too.

The 2018-19 edition of the Halifax Mooseheads, who finished runner-up in both the QMJHL and Memorial Cup finals, had 13 players from Atlantic Canada, including eight Nova Scotians.

The Rouyn-Noranda Huskies, based in Quebec, won both the league and Memorial Cup crowns with five Maritime players on the roster over the course of the season.

"I often wonder if we'd have a player like a Brad Marchand (without QMJHL expansion)," Reid says. "I think Sidney was going to be Sidney without that. But would we have had a Nathan without the Halifax Mooseheads?

"If the Mooseheads didn't come in 1994, would we have this skilled version of players we have now, because, when I look back, the guys who had to make it (did so by being) a grinder. That's probably because guys from Nova Scotia had to leave home, they had to go to Quebec, or out West, or to Ontario, to play major junior. They probably had to fight. And once you fight, you have to establish yourself as a grinder, because that's who you are."

The NHL has taken notice too. In 2005, Crosby became the first Nova Scotian drafted first overall. Since then, a handful of players from the Maritimes have been taken in the first round. Others include MacKinnon; James Sheppard of Lower Sackville, Nova Scotia; Logan MacMillan and Brandon Gormley of Prince Edward Island; and Zack Phillips and Noah Dobson from New Brunswick.

"I remember back in the day if a kid from Nova Scotia got drafted, you'd be like, 'Oh!'" Cossar says. "Now if we don't see a kid drafted in the first couple of rounds we're going, 'What's wrong?'

"If you're a top player, you're going to get found now. If there is a message from this for the kids, when you look at Nathan and Sidney, they were going to make it. But for others, you don't have to (leave Nova Scotia). If you do the work, the opportunities are there and you're going to be found. Because of the business it is today, they're not going to miss. (Scouts) make some mistakes, but for the most part they don't miss."

ALL-TIME POINTS LEADERS FROM NOVA SCOTIA
– according to quanthockey.com.

		GP	P
1	Al MacInnis, Port Hood	1,416	1,274
2	Sidney Crosby, Cole Harbour	943	1,216
3	Bobby Smith, North Sydney	1,077	1,036
4	Paul MacLean, Antigonish	719	673
5	Glen Murray, Bridgewater	1,009	651
6	Brad Marchand, Hammonds Plains	681	559
7	Nathan MacKinnon, Cole Harbour	456	402
8	Mike McPhee, River Bourgeois	744	390
9	Lowell MacDonald, New Glasgow	506	390
10	Doug Sulliman, Glace Bay	631	328

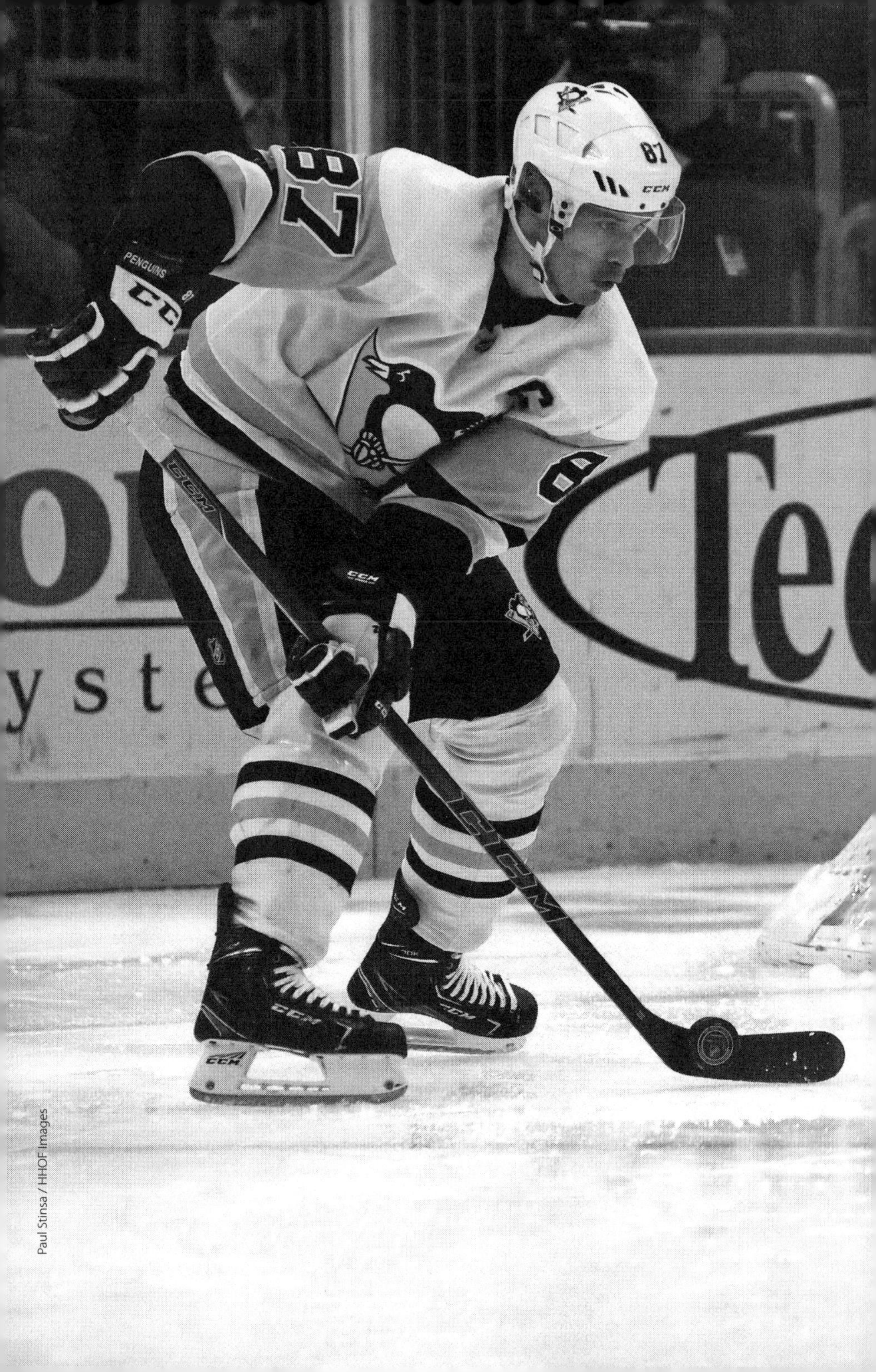

Paul Stinsa / HHOF Images

"He represents everything that is great about the game. When you look at him, he reveres the game. He respects it. He's also really down to earth, a Nova Scotian at heart . . . I don't think there are enough words to say all of the positives of him."

— Darren Cossar on Sidney Crosby

(Previous pages) Sidney Crosby of the Pittsburgh Penguins controls the puck near Corey Crawford of the Chicago Blackhawks during a game on December 12, 2018 at the United Center in Chicago.

CHAPTER 2
THE SIDNEY CROSBY STORY
From Phenom to Superstar

Brad Crossley laughs when asked what it was like coaching Sidney Crosby.

The former major midget coach of the Dartmouth Subways, Crossley had a front-row seat during Crosby's remarkable season with the club in 2001-02. Then-14-year-old Sid the Kid, as he was referred to for many more years, finished with a staggering 193 points in 74 games, including 95 goals.

"Sadly, I was too busy being a coach and not enough of being a fan," Crossley says, laughing as he reflects on that incredible season. "I was trying to drive him and get our team going at the same time. He drove the bus, even though he was so young."

Crosby has been driving the bus for teams since he first stepped onto the ice.

He was a hockey phenom at age 5, doing circles around his fellow Timbit players during scrimmages at Cole Harbour Place.

"His skill level at five, I had never seen anything like that," Paul Gallagher, running the Timbits program at the time, said in an interview for the 2013 book *Road to the NHL*.

"What amazed me about him is he had this great balance, and he could actually weave with the puck."

As Crosby moved up in minor hockey, so did his dominance. He put up point totals in the hundreds for the Cole Harbour Red Wings in atom, peewee and bantam AAA.

Crosby was so good, that by 13 (when most players are in second-year peewee), he made the Subways of the Nova Scotia Major Midget Hockey League. A legal fight over his age meant he couldn't actually play for them until 14.

Darren Cossar remembers the rumblings about Crosby as a minor-hockey phenom while working with Hockey Nova Scotia. He was so intrigued to see what this kid was about that he went and watched him play when Crosby was eight years old.

"He was different," Cossar says. "The line a lot of people use is the puck followed him. He understood the game so much more than any other kid. … He would get to where the puck was going before anybody. That was kind of special to see. Again, why would I go to a minor hockey game to watch a kid play? But again, as a hockey person, and you hear people talking about him, well, you have to go see."

'THE NEXT WAYNE GRETZKY'

It was with the Subways that Crosby enjoyed his first taste of the national spotlight. The Air Canada Cup national midget AAA hockey championships took place in Bathurst, New Brunswick in 2002 and

Crosby dominated. He finished with 24 points, including 11 goals, and was named tournament MVP. Dartmouth ended up losing out in the championship final, but Crosby became a national star.

"I can't imagine the pressure growing up that he would have been under, again, because he was really the first of that real skillset of players coming through Nova Scotia," Cossar says of the talk and hype about No. 87. "There were expectations at a very young age that he was going to be the next Wayne Gretzky. I can't imagine having that pressure and dealing with that. That speaks volumes to his family, the support he had, and him as a young man."

To help get away from this pressure, Crosby, then 15, packed his bags for Shattuck-St. Mary's, a prep school in Faribault, Minnesota, 90 kilometres south of the Twin Cities. He practised five days a week there, and got to play against older players, including U.S. junior A clubs and Division 3 colleges.

Crosby was a star at Shattuck, finishing with 162 points, including 72 goals, in 57 games as the squad went on to capture the national midget title.

"There were a lot of people saying he was going to be the next Gretzky, the next Mario Lemieux, the next Mark Messier, the next Brian Trottier all wrapped into one. That's pretty heavy stuff for a 15-year-old kid from Cole Harbour," Tom Ward, who ran the Shattuck-St. Mary's program for many years, said about Crosby in *Road to the NHL*.

Crosby announced his intentions to play in the QMJHL in May 2003 and a few weeks later was selected first overall by the Rimouski Oceanic. Like in every league before, Crosby was unstoppable as a junior. He finished his two years in Rimouski with 120 goals and 303 points in 121 games. He also led the Oceanic to the QMJHL title in 2005 and a spot in the four-team Memorial Cup.

By the end of that season, everyone knew he was ready to make the jump to the NHL.

Sidney Crosby was drafted by the QMJHL's Rimouski Oceanic in 2003 and led the team to the QMJHL title in 2005.

NO. 1, NO DOUBT

Everyone also knew Crosby would be going No. 1 in that 2005 NHL draft. What people didn't know was which team. The league was coming off a season-long lockout and a lottery the week before the draft determined the selection order.

Crosby's stardom had grown so much that a large group of reporters and photographers stood patiently outside his family's home that summer as he watched the proceedings with family and friends inside.

All 30 teams were in the running for the first pick. It came down to the Anaheim Mighty Ducks and the Pittsburgh Penguins. At 5:20 p.m., a loud cheer erupted inside the Crosby home. The Penguins had won.

"It was a lot of suspense going down the stretch," an emotionally spent Crosby, still only 17 at the time, told reporters on his front lawn on what was a warm July night. "It was just a lot of excitement, a lot of anticipation. It was definitely special."

As predicted, Crosby has become one of the best to lace them up in the NHL.

After being drafted by the Penguins first overall, he made the team as an 18-year-old and netted 39 goals and 102 points as a rookie. He followed that up with a career-best 120 points in his second season, winning both the Art Ross Trophy as the NHL scoring leader and Hart Memorial Trophy as league MVP. He remains the youngest winner (19) of the two awards.

Since then, he's won three Stanley Cups, recorded five more 100-point seasons and lived up to the expectations placed on him as the next big hockey superstar.

"What's fantastic about Sid, in just seeing his development over the years, he's not only a terrific offensive player, but he might be the best two-way player in the game right now," Crossley says. "He's developed his defensive end of the game. One of his favourite players was Steve Yzerman, and his game went that way as well. Sid just adds so many different dimensions to his game. He's doing everything, he's even killing penalties."

He also makes those around him better. In Chicago, Jonathan Toews has Patrick Kane. In Washington, Alex Ovechkin has Nicklas Backstrom. Crosby's linemates throughout the years? Chris Kunitz, Pascal Dupuis, Conor Sheary

Sidney Crosby enjoys a quiet moment during dryland warmup before a game on December 14, 2017 at T-Mobile Arena in Las Vegas.

Josh Holmberg/Hockey Hall of Fame

and Jake Guentzel to name but a few – good NHL players, but by no means stars.

"I think the way he lifts other players, that is the thing Sidney has on Nathan and Brad," Reid says. "You can put anybody on his line and he'll get him his points and make them better. You could throw anyone on Gretzky's wing and they produced. I think make Sid makes other players around him so much better. That's a valuable asset to have for a team."

Another valuable asset? Crosby's unmatched work ethic.

"I think Sidney Crosby is a fourth-line superstar," said Reid. "No one works harder than Sidney Crosby. It's impossible to take the puck from him in the corner, with the power he has.

"I think it's something people may overlook with Sid, that you can put anyone out there with him and he has a chance to make it work."

THE GOLDEN GOAL

Crosby has also shone on the international stage, most notably the famous "Golden Goal" for Canada at the 2010 Olympics in Vancouver. Coming on the heels of a disappointing seventh-place finish at the 2006 Winter Games in Turin, the pressure was on Team Canada to win gold in front of its home fans.

Crosby cemented his place among the game's greats by scoring the overtime winner for Canada against the United States in the gold medal final on Feb. 28, 2010. Crosby took a feed from the side boards from Jarome Iginla, then fired the puck between the legs of American netminder Ryan Miller.

After scoring, Crosby threw his gloves into the air and was mobbed by his Canadian teammates. The Golden Goal as it's now famously referred to has been shown countless times over the past decade and can still bring a chill to the spine watching it.

Sidney Crosby celebrates his game-winning goal during overtime in the men's gold medal hockey game at the 2010 Winter Olympic Games in Vancouver, on Feb. 28, 2010. Known as the Golden Goal, it helped cement Crosby's place in Canadian hockey history.

THE CANADIAN PRESS/Paul Chiasson

Sidney Crosby chats with some of the kids at his second annual hockey school at Cole Harbour Place on July 11, 2016.

"Looking back on that moment, there's every bit a special feeling that comes with every time I talk about it or every time somebody brings it up," Crosby said in a CBC story from 2017 reliving that historic goal. "It doesn't get any less satisfying or anything like that. It's a special moment. I love that moment. That's something I'll have forever. It's not going anywhere."

Crosby is now in the latter stages of his career. He turned 32 in August and is entering his 15th NHL season, which includes his much publicized issues with concussions from 2011 to 2016 that forced him out of action for lengthy periods of time. Along with his three Stanley Cup rings, he has two playoff MVP trophies, two Olympic gold medals – the list goes on and on.

But with everything he's accomplished and endured, the people who know him best say he's not close to being done.

"I think it's stronger than it's ever been," Crossley says of his desire to win.

"He's made a couple comments to me over the last couple of summers, 'Geez Cros, I'm not as young as I once was.' I think because of that, he's a little more cognizant of his rest-to-work ratio. But his work ethic is probably as high as it's ever been right now. He just loves the game so much and he wants to make an impact and he wants to win."

CROSBY: SUPERSTAR, MENTOR

Sidney Crosby has become a mentor to countless young hockey players, including that other Cole Harbour superstar.

Crosby has had a big influence on Nathan MacKinnon the past few years, helping to show him the way both on and off the ice as a professional.

The two are very good friends, despite an eight-year age gap. The two train together throughout the summer, with MacKinnon even building a home right next to Crosby's in the Halifax suburb of Grand Lake.

There are also the pair's commercials for Tim Hortons, drawing laughs and attention from coast to coast.

"They are best buddies," Crossley says. "Sid has taken him under his wing a little bit the last couple of years, calm him down and show him how to be a professional. I think Nathan is better because of it. He's always looked up to Sid. They've developed a great friendship. They train religiously together. ... They're best buddies in the off season. But when you see them in practice together, you would never know they were friends."

Sidney Crosby hoists the Stanley Cup after a parade in his hometown of Cole Harbour, Nova Scotia on Friday, August 7, 2009.

CAREER NHL STATS

	GP	G	A	P
2005-06	81	39	63	102
2006-07	79	36	84	120
2007-08	53	24	48	72
2008-09	77	33	70	103
2009-10	81	51	58	109
2010-11	41	32	34	66
2011-12	22	8	29	37
2012-13	36	15	41	56
2013-14	80	36	68	104
2014-15	77	28	56	84
2015-16	80	36	49	85
2016-17	75	44	45	89
2017-18	82	29	60	89
2018-19	79	35	65	100
TOTALS	943	446	770	1,216

Source: NHL.com

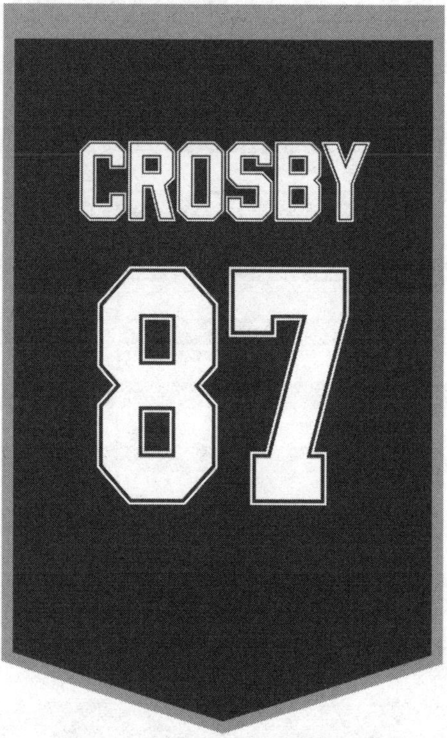
CROSBY
87

CHAPTER 3
SIDNEY CROSBY'S SEASON

Going into the 2018-19 season, Sidney Crosby had gone four years without reaching the 100-point plateau.

He was putting up good offensive numbers at more than a point per game – but from 2014-18, he was never able to surpass 90 points.

When looking at his 2018-19 season, it's interesting to note that he was held off the scoresheet in 24 of the 79 games he played in but recorded more than a point per game 32 times. In fact, it was multiple-point games in Games 81 and 82 of the regular season that propelled Crosby to his sixth 100-point season.

Sidney Crosby and the Edmonton Oilers' Connor McDavid in a November 2017 game at Rogers Place in Edmonton.

The following is a month-by-month breakdown of how he got to 100.

OCTOBER – 14 points in 10 games

After recording five points in six games to begin the season, Crosby really heated up during a road trip to western Canada. He finished the three games against the Edmonton Oilers, Calgary Flames and Vancouver Canucks with five goals and two assists.

The best goal of the trip – maybe the entire NHL season – came against the Oilers on Oct. 23. During 3-on-3 overtime, a vintage Crosby skated the puck into the offensive zone, danced around an Oilers defenceman, then brought the puck to the front of the net and put a back-hander past goaltender Cam Talbot. It was his second goal of the game – and his first two of the season – in what was a highly anticipated showdown between No. 87 and Oilers superstar Connor McDavid.

"Listen, I'm not changing the way I play," Crosby told reporters after the game about the marquee matchup. "I'm going out there every night to try and create things and come up with big plays when they're needed. There's a lot of us that want to do that on every single team, who look to do that. I'm not any different than [McDavid] is as far as understanding my responsibility and wanting to be at my best."

OCTOBER	G	A	P	Shifts	Ice Time
4 – vs. Washington	0	2	2	25	22:01
6 – vs. Montreal	0	0	0	21	18:38
11 – vs. Las Vegas	0	1	1	20	16:44
13 – at Montreal	0	1	1	30	21:54
16 – vs. Vancouver	0	0	0	24	21:07
18 – at Toronto	0	1	1	27	19:40
23 – at Edmonton	2	0	2	27	20:33
25 – at Calgary	1	2	3	20	16:54
27 – at Vancouver	2	0	2	24	20:03
30 – vs. N.Y. Islanders	1	1	2	24	20:21
Source: NHL.com					

NOVEMBER – 14 points in 11 games

NOVEMBER	G	A	P	Shifts	Ice Time
1 – at N.Y. Islanders	0	0	0	28	24:23
3 – vs. Toronto	0	0	0	26	20:37
5 – vs. New Jersey	0	0	0	22	20:22
7 – at Washington	1	0	1	26	21:35
10 – vs. Arizona	1	1	2	20	16:54
13 – at New Jersey	0	2	2	27	21:32
21 – vs. Dallas	1	2	3	23	16:54
23 – at Boston	0	0	0	31	23:12
24 – vs. Columbus	0	2	2	28	20:36
27 – at Winnipeg	1	0	1	26	20:07
28 – at Colorado	3	0	3	26	20:44
Source: NHL.com					

November started off slowly for Crosby as he was held off the scoresheet in games against the New York Islanders, Toronto Maple Leafs and New Jersey Devils. But Crosby heated up the rest of the month, finishing with 14 points in his final eight games.

That included a goal and two assists against the Dallas Stars on Nov. 21, and a natural hat trick in Colorado against Nathan MacKinnon and the Avalanche on Nov. 28.

The three-goal game was his lone hat trick of the season and 11th of his career. It included a breakaway marker, a goal from a bad angle, and driving the net scoring on a rebound from in close. It should be noted MacKinnon finished with four points and was named first star in a 6-3 Avalanche win.

DECEMBER – 20 points in 15 games

This was the best offensive month for Crosby. He played in 15 games and had multiple points seven times. What's more impressive is that Crosby started the month with only four points in six games, and then went on a tear, recording 16 points in nine games.

He was at his hottest as 2018 came to a close. He finished with 10 points in four games, including a goal and two assists against the St. Louis Blues on Dec. 29 and a goal and an assist against the Minnesota Wild on Dec. 31.

Another interesting tidbit: Crosby's two-point performance against Minnesota came in his 900th NHL game.

DECEMBER	G	A	P	Shifts	Ice Time
1 – vs. Philadelphia	1	0	1	24	20:05
4 – vs. Colorado	0	0	0	28	19:46
6 – vs. N.Y. Islanders	1	2	3	24	22:19
8 – at Ottawa	0	0	0	23	20:13
10 – at N.Y. Islanders	0	0	0	27	23:56
12 – at Chicago	0	0	0	25	22:58
14 – vs. Boston	0	2	2	27	21:05
15 – vs. L.A. Kings	0	1	1	28	22:55
17 – vs. Anaheim	0	1	1	26	21:04
19 – at Washington	1	1	2	25	22:07
20 – vs. Minnesota	0	0	0	24	19:45
22 – at Carolina	0	3	3	28	20:34
27 – vs. Detroit	0	2	2	23	20:04
29 – at St. Louis	1	2	3	25	18:13
31 – at Minnesota	1	1	2	28	19:56

Source: NHL.com

JANUARY – 10 points in 11 games

JANUARY	G	A	P	Shifts	Ice Time
2 – at N.Y. Rangers	1	1	2	24	19:10
4 – vs. Winnipeg	0	1	1	24	21:47
6 – vs. Chicago	0	0	0	23	20:28
8 – vs. Florida	1	1	2	24	20:44
11 – at Anaheim	0	1	1	26	22:05
12 – at Los Angeles	0	1	1	27	23:46
15 – at San Jose	0	0	0	26	21:11
18 – at Arizona	0	1	1	29	21:54
19 – at Vegas	1	0	1	25	20:41
28 – at New Jersey	0	0	0	25	20:32
31 – vs. Tampa Bay	1	0	1	26	22:00
Source: NHL.com					

This was a cooler month point-wise for Crosby, who had only two multiple-point games – a goal and an assist against the Rangers on Jan. 2 and a goal and an assist against the Florida Panthers on Jan. 8. He finished the month with four goals, including one against the Tampa Bay Lightning on Jan. 30 when he and Phil Kessel scored first-period markers just 16 seconds apart.

While it doesn't count in his point total, Crosby also played in the NHL all-star game in San Jose on Jan. 27. Crosby and the Metropolitan Division came out on top, with No. 87 finishing with four goals and eight points and was named MVP. It's the first time he accomplished that feat in his career.

"I feel pretty good about my game. The consistency has been there," Crosby told reporters afterwards about his season to date. "I think as a line we've been strong at both ends of the ice, the speed, creating things on a nightly basis."

FEBRUARY – 19 points in 13 games

Crosby was back to producing more than a point per game in February. In 13 games, he had six multiple-point contests, and finished with three points three times.

He had a goal and two assists on Feb. 11 against the Philadelphia Flyers and again on Feb. 16 against Calgary. He also had three assists on Feb. 17 against the Rangers.

Crosby had 77 points with 19 games remaining when the month ended, putting him on pace for more than 100 points.

FEBRUARY	G	A	P	Shifts	Ice Time
1 – vs. Ottawa	0	2	2	22	21:07
2 – at Toronto	1	0	1	26	20:24
5 – vs. Carolina	0	0	0	21	22:46
7 – vs. Florida	0	0	0	28	21:57
9 – at Tampa Bay	0	1	1	32	22:37
11 – at Philadelphia	1	2	3	27	20:53
13 – vs. Edmonton	0	1	1	23	20:36
16 – vs. Calgary	1	2	3	24	21:35
17 – vs. N.Y. Rangers	0	3	3	24	21:41
19 – at New Jersey	0	1	1	26	19:24
21 – vs. San Jose	0	0	0	23	19:08
23 – at Philadelphia	1	1	2	28	20:19
26 – at Columbus	1	1	2	29	22:02

Source: NHL.com

MARCH	G	A	P	Shifts	Ice Time
1 – at Buffalo	1	1	2	30	22:13
2 – at Montreal	1	3	4	27	19:06
5 – vs. Florida	1	2	3	30	21:47
7 – vs. Columbus	1	0	1	27	20:35
9 – at Columbus	0	0	0	27	20:00
10 – vs. Boston	0	1	1	29	21:48
12 – vs. Washington	2	0	2	29	21:25
14 – at Buffalo	0	2	2	24	22:21
16 – vs. St. Louis	0	0	0	23	20:51
17 – vs. Philadelphia	0	0	0	33	24:11
19 – at Carolina	0	1	1	31	20:49
21 – at Nashville	0	0	0	29	23:41
23 – at Dallas	0	0	0	26	19:39
25 – at N.Y. Rangers	0	1	1	25	20:04
29 – vs. Nashville	0	0	0	24	24:31
31 – vs. Carolina	0	0	0	27	22:42
Source: NHL.com					

MARCH – 17 points in 16 games

Crosby came out of the gates flying in the final full month of the regular season. He had nine points in three games to begin March, including a goal and three assists against the Montreal Canadiens on March 2, then a goal and two helpers at home to the Panthers on March 5.

He cooled down a bit – with six points in his next five games – but was sitting at 92 points with 11 games remaining.

Then came his worst offensive stretch of the season – two assists in eight games – to sit at 94 points with only three games left.

Suddenly, getting to 100 points went from being a formality to a long shot for No. 87.

APRIL – 6 points in 3 games

Great players rise to the occasion and that's exactly what Crosby did over those final three games to reach 100 points.

After getting an assist on April 2 in Detroit to reach 95 points, Crosby played at home for the final two games and made the most of them.

He had a goal and two assists on April 4 against the Red Wings, pushing him to 98 points with one game left against the Rangers. Crosby recorded point 99 in the first period, when he took a feed from Guentzel and one-timed a shot off the goal post and in. It looked like Crosby might be stuck at 99, but with less than three minutes to go in the third period, he dug out a loose puck in front of the Rangers net and Guentzel was able to put in his 40th goal of the season with the assist from Sid.

"Congratulations Jake. Congratulations Sidney Crosby," was how Penguins color commentator Bob Errey symbolized the moment. In his typical humble fashion, Crosby didn't once mention getting to 100 points to media afterwards. He talked instead about getting ready for the playoffs and that game-tying goal by Guentzel.

By reaching 100 points for the sixth time in his career, Crosby now sits in a tie for sixth for the most times by one player in NHL history. Leading the pack is Wayne Gretzky, who accomplished the feat an amazing 15 times in 20 seasons.

APRIL	G	A	P	Shifts	Ice Time
2 – at Detroit	0	1	1	25	20:46
4 – vs. Detroit	1	2	3	24	20:57
6 – vs. N.Y. Rangers	1	1	2	24	22:17
Source: NHL.com					

MOST 100-POINT SEASONS, NHL CAREER	
Wayne Gretzky	15 (20 seasons)
Mario Lemieux	10 (17 seasons)
Marcel Dionne	8 (18 seasons)
Mike Bossy	7 (10 seasons)
Peter Stastny	7 (15 seasons)
T-6. Bobby Orr	6 (12 seasons)
T-6. Sidney Crosby	6 (14 seasons)
T-6. Dale Hawerchuk	6 (16 seasons)
T-6. Jari Kurri	6 (17 seasons)
T-6. Guy Lafleur	6 (17 seasons)
T-6. Phil Esposito	6 (18 seasons)
T-6. Brian Trottier	6 (18 seasons)
T-6. Joe Sakic	6 (20 seasons)
T-6. Steve Yzerman	6 (22 seasons)
T-6. Mark Messier	6 (25 seasons)
Source: NHL.com	

Dave Sandford / HHOF Images

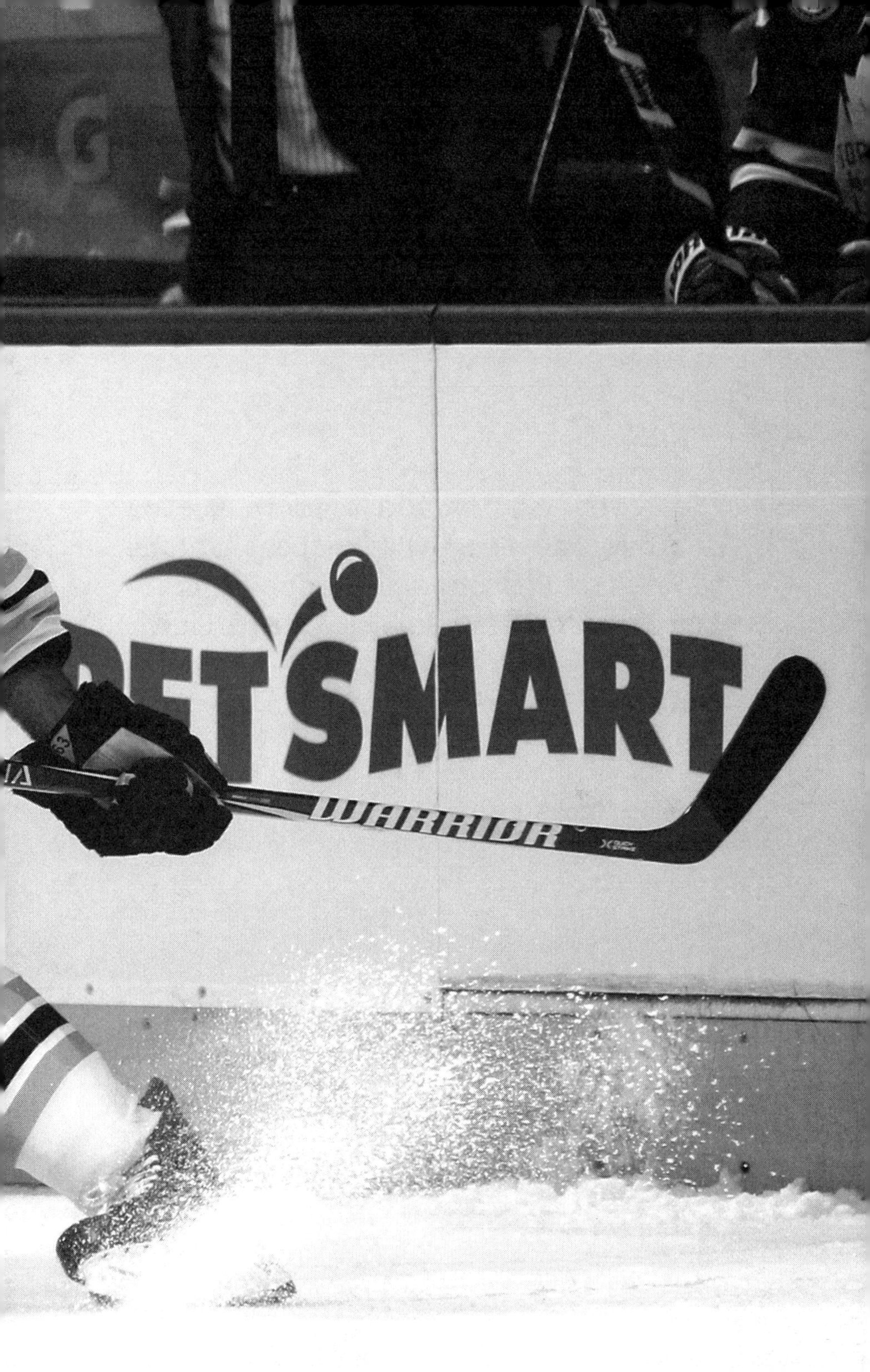
SMART
WARRIOR

"He loves leading his team in Boston. He loves getting the respect of the people in Boston. They love him. And I don't think he compares himself to (Crosby and MacKinnon). He just wants to be the best he can be for his team."

— Brad Crossley

(Previous pages) Brad Marchand of the Boston Bruins looks on during 2017 Hockey Hall of Fame Game action against the Toronto Maple Leafs at the Air Canada Centre in Toronto on November 10, 2017.

CHAPTER 4
THE BRAD MARCHAND STORY
Bulldog Makes It as a Bruin

If you like an underdog, Brad Marchand is your guy.

While he always stood out as a top offensive player from minor hockey through to four years of junior, few believed Marchand would become the NHL star he is today.

Marchand always believed he could make it and was driven to prove the naysayers wrong. Marchand has said even some members of his own family thought he was simply too small, and not talented enough to become the NHLer he is today.

"He was a guy, we'd all go, 'He'd be a captain of a university team. Might be a captain in the minor leagues of the American league,'" Darren Cossar says of how Marchand had been viewed in Nova Scotia hockey circles growing up. "A good hockey player, determined, who had that grit and edge.

Brad Marchand during a preseason game on September 25, 2017 at the TD Garden in Boston.

"I think he was one of a bunch ... they could be (future NHLers). ... And I think you felt that right up to when he made the NHL full time. That's not a knock against him, it's a credit to his determination. He's a guy who found his niche and honed his skills to become a lot more than what anyone had thought."

Born and raised in Hammonds Plains, Marchand began playing minor hockey in the Bedford Minor Hockey Association, before switching to the neighbouring TASA Minor Hockey Association.

'LIKE A BULLDOG OUT THERE'

Always on the AAA teams for minor hockey, Marchand showed a knack for scoring, and when peewee rolled around, he took a liking to body checking.

"I would just run around and hit guys all game," Marchand said of his time in peewee in an interview for the book *Road to the NHL*. "I didn't even care about the puck. The only thing I wanted to do was hit guys. That's where it started."

By "it," he's referring to that in-your-face, pest style of game he mastered in the NHL, and has gone too far with at times.

Marchand really began to find his game in bantam AAA as he recorded more than 90 goals and 150 points in one season. He was now catching the eye of the city's major midget programs, most notably the Subways.

Brad Marchand and a loose puck attract the attention of MacKenzie Weegar and Bogdan Kiselevich of the Florida Panthers during a game on December 4, 2018 at BB&T Centre in Sunrise, Florida.

In Dartmouth, Marchand enjoyed another great year, finishing with 47 goals and 94 points to lead the powerhouse Subways in scoring. Even as an undersized player in midget, he played without fear.

"Brad was like a bulldog out there, going in the corners and shooting pucks," says Crossley, who coached Marchand for his only season in Dartmouth.

Brad Marchand shows off his gold medal, after an overtime win against Sweden at the 2008 IIHF World Junior Championship. Marchand has represented Canada four times in the 2007, 2008 World Junior Hockey Championships, 2016 IIHF World Championships, and 2016 World Cup of Hockey bringing home gold from each tournament. He scored the winning goal for Canada, short-handed, in the second and deciding game of the 2016 World Cup of Hockey final. He was the tournament's top goal-scorer and named to the all-star team.

Mikael Fritzon / HHOF-IIHF Images

"A lot of people don't like Brad's game, but I'd take him on my team any time. His teammates love him because he's a team-first guy and he contributes. Brad plays like he's six-foot-three on a five-foot-nine frame."

When the QMJHL draft rolled around, Marchand was hoping to be selected in the first round. Instead, he was taken in the second round by the Moncton Wildcats. He went to training camp and earned a spot on the club as a 16-year-old.

Marchand excelled as a junior. He helped the Wildcats win the QMJHL title in the 2005-06 season and twice played for Canada at the World Junior Hockey Championships – both times bringing home gold.

"I think he came into his own the last two years of junior and realized his potential," Crossley says. "He took his game to another level once he became a pro."

SLOWER ROAD TO THE TOP

Marchand was taken in the third round by the Bruins in the 2006 NHL draft. He turned professional in 2008 after signing an entry-level contract with Boston. He didn't make the Bruins out of training camp and was assigned to the team's AHL affiliate in Providence. Always seeing himself as a top guy, the demotion was initially hard, but Marchand soon realized how much it was needed.

"Looking back at it, nothing better could've happened for me as a player," he said in *Road to the NHL*. "I grew so much. I learned so much being there."

Rob Murray was Marchand's coach for that first season in Providence. He told Metro Halifax in a 2009 interview that Marchand came into his office one day and told him, "I want you to make me a man as a hockey player."

Marchand went out and had a tremendous regular season, finishing with 59 points in 79 games. He was also named the team's rookie of the year.

He would start his second professional season in Providence but was one of the NHL team's last cuts at training camp. He knew he was getting closer to the NHL.

He wasn't in the minors for much longer. After scoring seven goals in his first 15 games, the Bruins called up Marchand to make his NHL debut on Oct. 21, 2009 against the Nashville Predators. Marchand couldn't stick, however, and was sent down, called up and sent down again. He finished the 2009-10 season with 20 games for the Bruins.

The next year at camp, Marchand made the team from the outset. When he finally scored his first NHL goal on Nov. 3, 2010 in Buffalo – in what was his 29th NHL game – his confidence grew and so did his game. He hasn't slowed down since.

"I needed a couple of recalls before I finally got it," Marchand said in *Road to the NHL*. "And I never really got it until about halfway through 2010-11."

Marchand has developed into one of the game's best players. He is on Boston's top line, top power play unit and No. 1 penalty-killing duo. His point totals have been increasing almost every season as well. He recorded a career-best 61 points during the 2015-16 campaign. He jumped to 85 points in each of the next two years and followed that up by reaching 100 in the 2018-19 season.

"I think that's where you've seen a transition in Brad. He really had to play with an edge, he was undersized. But that is going and you're seeing his skill more and more as the game has changed in the last couple of years," Cossar says.

"He had to be a little more aggressive, he had to have that edge to get some space. Under the new game and the way it is, you don't necessarily need that. Your skill will allow you to thrive in the game."

Brad Marchand hoists the Stanley Cup for a throng of fans gathered at Grand Parade in Halifax on Tuesday, Aug. 30, 2011.

PLAYING ON THE EDGE

Of course, you can't talk about Marchand without bringing up his on-ice antics. He's most infamously remembered for twice licking the faces of players during the 2018 Stanley Cup playoffs. He's been suspended in the regular season six times for a total of 19 games, including two suspensions worth five games apiece. He's also been fined five times by the NHL for five separate incidents, costing him more than $24,000.

"If you look at it from the outside, I'd be like, 'Oh, God. Don't do that Brad.' But on the other side of that, when you get to know him and you see that why Brad is so good is that edge," Cossar says. "He has to play on that edge or he's not going to be successful.

"Unfortunately, with that you every now and then go over that edge. But what I've seen from Brad, is the maturity of him over the period of time, from when he broke in and won that first Stanley

Cup, to today. The things I've seen from him away from the rink – he's a real genuine good guy at heart."

Marchand doesn't apologize for playing on the edge. It's the way he's always played and fans in Boston love him for it. Outside of Boston, he's arguably the most hated player in the NHL but is also someone every team in the league would love to have.

"I think having Brad Marchand on your team would be awesome," Ken Reid says. "I love that he has personality. I love that he's not afraid to take it too far sometimes. Obviously, when you play that game, you're going to cross the line. I love that he's willing to do whatever it takes to get into someone's grill. And I think he kind of enjoys that, which I like.

Brad Marchand, David Pastrnak, Patrice Bergeron and David Krejci celebrate a goal during a game against the Winnipeg Jets on March 27, 2018 at the Bell MTS Place in Winnipeg.

"I know it rubs a lot of people the wrong way, but I like what he's doing. If that's what he has to do to get 100 points and make it all the way to the Stanley Cup final, then that is what he has to do. The other guys do other things, but that's what works for him. He's obviously figured it out. It's working."

Brad Marchand during a game against the Winnipeg Jets on March 14, 2019 at Bell MTS Place in Winnipeg.

More importantly, his teammates love and appreciate his skill, work ethic and the leadership he brings to the ice each game. They also enjoy watching him become an NHL superstar.

"It's all from his own doing," linemate Patrice Bergeron said about Marchand during an interview for the Bruins last season.

"I couldn't be any happier and prouder for him. Everything he's put in and all the time and the effort has paid off. You could see over the last few years he was becoming really an elite player in this league, and one of the best left wingers. He's proven that again this year."

'WE HAD A HELL OF A YEAR'

Brad Marchand was so close to becoming a two-time Stanley Cup champion.

After helping the Bruins win their first Cup in 39 years back in 2011, Marchand and the Bruins looked to be on the verge of winning Lord Stanley's mug again in 2019. But the club couldn't put away the St. Louis Blues in the Stanley Cup final despite holding a 3-2 series edge. In Game 7, the Bruins were blanked 4-0 at home and endured the pain of watching St. Louis celebrate on the TD Garden ice.

Marchand couldn't hold back his disappointment. A photo of him crying on the ice after the loss went viral. Marchand later said the setback was by far the worst of his career.

"I love these guys," a somber Marchand told reporters after that Game 7. "We had a hell of a year. We came very close. I love every guy on this team and I'm very proud of everyone. They worked their ass off all year to get to this point. We came together, we're like a family. It hurts."

Cossar wasn't surprised to see how much that loss hurt Marchand.

"I think that's where his focus is now. You see the players when they get to that level, it's about Cups," Cossar says. "You see great players who don't get the credit they deserve because they never won a Cup. That was some of the emotion you saw at the end this year. You saw someone who knows you don't get many of those chances."

Val-d'Or Foreurs' forward Brad Marchand from Hammonds Plains carries the puck up the ice against the Halifax Mooseheads during the first period of QMJHL action at the Metro Centre on October 27, 2006.

Ryan Taplin photo

Brad Marchand gives a puck to one of his young fans during the warm up prior to a game on March 27, 2018 at the Bell MTS Place in Winnipeg.

Rusty Barton/Hockey Hall of Fame

CAREER NHL STATS

	GP	G	A	P
2009-10	20	0	1	1
2010-11	77	21	20	41
2011-12	76	28	27	55
2012-13	45	18	18	36
2013-14	82	25	28	53
2014-15	77	24	18	42
2015-16	77	37	24	61
2016-17	80	39	46	85
2017-18	68	34	51	85
2018-19	79	36	64	100
TOTALS	681	262	297	559

Source: NHL.com

MARCHAND

63

CHAPTER 5
BRAD MARCHAND'S SEASON

Two things are required to reach the 100-point milestone: good health and offensive consistency.

In 2017-18, Marchand averaged 1.25 points per game and could have hit the elusive 100 target. But injuries totaling nine games, plus a five-game suspension for an elbow to the head of New Jersey Devils forward Marcus Johannson on Jan. 23, made that impossible.

He still tied his career-high in points with 85 that year and improved on his play-making skills with a career-best 51 assists.

So getting to 100 points was a real possibility for Marchand in 2018-19. But he needed to stay healthy and not get another suspension. Marchand avoided both and was able to hit the century mark with two games to spare.

Here's a month-by-month breakdown of how he got to 100.

OCTOBER – 15 points in 12 games

After putting up a goose egg to open the regular season, Marchand caught fire with seven points in his next two contests. He had four assists against the Buffalo Sabres on Oct. 4 and then three helpers at home to the Ottawa Senators on Oct. 8.

He ended the month on a strong note with two goals against the Carolina Hurricanes on Oct. 30. It was his first multiple-goal game of the season after scoring just twice in the previous 11 contests. Against Carolina, Marchand scored on the power play, short-handed and was the game's first star.

"It's been a little tough, I don't think I'd really been pulling my weight," Marchand told reporters after the game on Oct. 30. "It was nice to get a couple tonight. It all starts with big plays from other guys. I was just the beneficiary."

OCTOBER	G	A	P	Shifts	Ice Time
3 – vs. Washington	0	0	0	20	14:56
4 – at Buffalo	0	4	4	22	17:10
8 – vs. Ottawa	0	3	3	25	18:47
11 – vs. Edmonton	1	0	1	24	20:19
13 – vs. Detroit	0	2	2	22	15:27
17 – at Calgary	1	0	1	24	20:32
18 – at Edmonton	0	1	1	24	21:33
20 – at Vancouver	0	0	0	26	23:52
23 – at Ottawa	0	1	1	23	15:06
25 – vs. Philadelphia	0	0	0	23	24:10
27 – vs. Montreal	0	0	0	27	21:00
30 – at Carolina	2	0	2	26	20:27

Source: NHL.com

NOVEMBER	G	A	P	Shifts	Ice Time
3 – at Nashville	0	0	0	21	18:21
5 – vs. Dallas	1	0	1	25	22:06
8 – vs. Vancouver	0	1	1	24	22:14
10 – vs. Toronto	0	2	2	23	18:38
11 – vs. Vegas	1	0	1	23	19:44
14 – at Colorado	0	0	0	23	18:53
16 – at Dallas	0	0	0	19	15:05
17 – at Arizona	0	1	1	23	21:37
21 – at Detroit	0	0	0	22	16:15
23 – vs. Pittsburgh	0	0	0	27	20:20
24 – at Montreal	0	0	0	21	19:57
26 – at Toronto	0	2	2	21	20:41
29 – vs. N.Y. Islanders	1	0	1	23	21:39
Source: NHL.com					

NOVEMBER – 9 points in 13 games

This was a tough month for Marchand as he was held off the scoresheet in six of 13 games. He also had only two multiple-point games.

One of those games came Nov. 26 in Toronto when Marchand had two assists against the Maple Leafs. He followed that up with his seventh goal of the season Nov. 29 at home against the New York Islanders.

He finished the first two months of the season with 24 points in 25 games, putting him on pace for only about 80 points.

DECEMBER – 17 points in 13 games

Marchand needed a great last month of 2018 to be in line for a 100-point season and he delivered.

Marchand didn't get a single point in the first three games in December but then he turned red hot. He went the final 10 games with 17 points, including three three-point games.

He had three assists Dec. 8 in Toronto, two goals and an assist at home to the Phoenix Coyotes on Dec. 11, and a goal and two helpers Dec. 23 against the Nashville Predators at TD Garden in Boston.

Against Nashville, Marchand's longtime friend and centre Patrice Bergeron scored his 300th NHL goal. Afterwards, Marchand referred to Bergeron as one of the NHL's best players.

DECEMBER	G	A	P	Shifts	Ice Time
1 – vs. Detroit	0	0	0	25	22:14
4 – at Florida	0	0	0	21	16:52
6 – at Tampa Bay	0	0	0	23	20:59
8 – vs. Toronto	0	3	3	26	20:16
9 – at Ottawa	1	1	2	23	23:39
11 – vs. Arizona	2	1	3	27	23:15
14 – at Pittsburgh	0	1	1	22	21:50
16 – vs. Buffalo	0	0	0	22	22:13
17 – at Montreal	1	0	1	23	18:44
20 – vs. Anaheim	0	2	2	23	18:42
22 – vs. Nashville	1	2	3	24	18:50
23 – at Carolina	0	2	2	26	22:30
27 – vs. New Jersey	0	0	0	23	20:20

Source: NHL.com

JANUARY	G	A	P	Shifts	Ice Time
1 – at Chicago	1	0	1	27	19:13
3 – vs. Calgary	2	0	2	24	18:27
5 – vs. Buffalo	0	0	0	21	19:58
8 – vs. Minnesota	1	2	3	18	12:47
10 – vs. Washington	0	0	0	22	23:01
12 – at Toronto	0	0	0	25	19:37
14 – vs. Montreal	1	1	2	23	18:26
16 – at Philadelphia	0	2	2	23	21:00
17 – vs. St. Louis	1	0	1	22	21:08
19 – vs. N.Y. Rangers	1	0	1	22	19:29
29 – vs. Winnipeg	0	3	3	27	20:25
31 – vs. Philadelphia	0	1	1	25	19:45

Source: NHL.com

JANUARY – 16 points in 12 games

It was another big month for Marchand.

After starting January with six points in six games, Marchand exploded offensively with 10 points in six contests.

That included a goal and an assist against the Montreal Canadiens on Jan. 14 and three assists Jan. 29 against the Winnipeg Jets.

Marchand had 57 points in 50 games when January ended, putting him in line to reach 100 points but it was by no means a sure thing.

FEBRUARY – 18 points in 13 games

If Marchand wasn't thinking about 100 before February, he was afterwards.

He finished the month with a total of six multiple-point games. That included a five-game stretch where he had 12 points. Marchand had two-point games Feb. 5 against the Islanders, Feb. 6 against the Rangers, Feb. 9 against the Los Angeles Kings and Feb. 10 against the Colorado Avalanche.

He followed up that stretch with his biggest offensive output of the season – a goal and three assists against the Chicago Blackhawks on Feb. 12.

"It's nice to win games like that," Marchand told reporters after the team's 6-3 home-ice win versus Chicago. "It doesn't happen often and it hasn't been the way we've been winning. You have to be able to win games like that. It's nice to win 'em like that. It was a fun one."

FEBRUARY	G	A	P	Shifts	Ice Time
3 – at Washington	0	0	0	21	20:04
5 – vs. N.Y. Islanders	0	2	2	21	17:49
6 – at N.Y. Rangers	0	2	2	25	19:29
9 – vs. Los Angeles	1	1	2	25	22:30
10 – vs. Colorado	1	1	2	24	18:52
12 – vs. Chicago	1	3	4	22	20:29
15 – at Anaheim	0	0	0	20	18:18
16 – at Los Angeles	1	0	1	22	17:44
18 – at San Jose	0	0	0	29	23:44
20 – at Vegas	1	0	1	21	21:11
23 – at St. Louis	0	0	0	24	19:39
26 – vs. San Jose	1	2	3	22	16:13
28 – vs. Tampa Bay	1	0	1	21	18:19

Source: NHL.com

MARCH	G	A	P	Shifts	Ice Time
2 – vs. New Jersey	1	0	1	20	18:47
5 – vs. Carolina	0	1	1	26	22:27
7 – vs. Florida	0	3	3	25	21:12
9 – vs. Ottawa	1	0	1	22	18:11
10 – at Pittsburgh	0	1	1	24	20:21
12 – at Columbus	2	1	3	24	21:22
14 – at Winnipeg	0	0	0	22	19:37
16 – vs. Columbus	1	1	2	27	21:44
19 – at N.Y. Islanders	0	0	0	20	15:32
21 – at New Jersey	0	3	3	18	15:54
23 – at Florida	1	1	2	22	18:01
25 – at Tampa Bay	2	0	2	23	17:02
27 – vs. N.Y. Rangers	0	3	3	20	19:46
30 – vs. Florida	0	0	0	21	16:53
31 – at Detroit	1	0	1	22	19:57

Source: NHL.com

MARCH – 23 points in 15 games

His biggest month of the season offensively made getting to 100 points seem almost like a formality.

Four three-point games, three two-point games and five one-point games put the forward at 98 points with three games remaining. His best stretch came between March 21 and 27 when he had 10 points over four games, including a two-goal performance against the league-leading Tampa Bay Lightning.

He ended the month with a short-handed goal against the Red Wings on March 31. It was Marchand's 26th career short-handed marker, beating the previous Bruins franchise record held by Rick Middleton.

APRIL – 2 points in 1 game

"Couldn't be prouder." Those were the words from Bruins head coach Bruce Cassidy to reporters after Marchand's goal and an assist against the Columbus Blue Jackets on April 2 to become the 10th Boston player in history to reach 100 points.

"He's worked really, really hard. I'm gonna guess he's worked as hard as anyone in the National Hockey League to round out his shot, his puck play," Cassidy said afterwards.

Marchand's 99th and 100th points came in quick succession. He scored his 36th goal of the season with about five minutes to play in the second period to hit point 99, then had the second assist on a marker by David Pastrnak just 37 seconds later to reach the century mark.

"I love you guys," Marchand could be heard on the ice telling his linemates behind the Blue Jackets net as they celebrated the goal and milestone. Marchand was the first Bruins player to reach 100 points since Joe Thornton did it back in 2002-03.

"It's a pretty good feeling, but I think it shows just how good a team we have," Marchand told reporters afterwards. "You know it's cool – it's a cool personal stat."

With their playoff position secured, Marchand didn't dress the final two regular-season games so he could get ready for the post-season. What a year it was for No. 63.

APRIL	G	A	P	Shifts	Ice Time
2 – at Columbus	1	1	2	20	16:40
Source: NHL.com					

Brad Marchand in a Stanley Cup parade in downtown Halifax on Aug. 29, 2011, as it heads past the Old Clock Tower on Citadel Hill.

Perry Nelson / HHOF Images

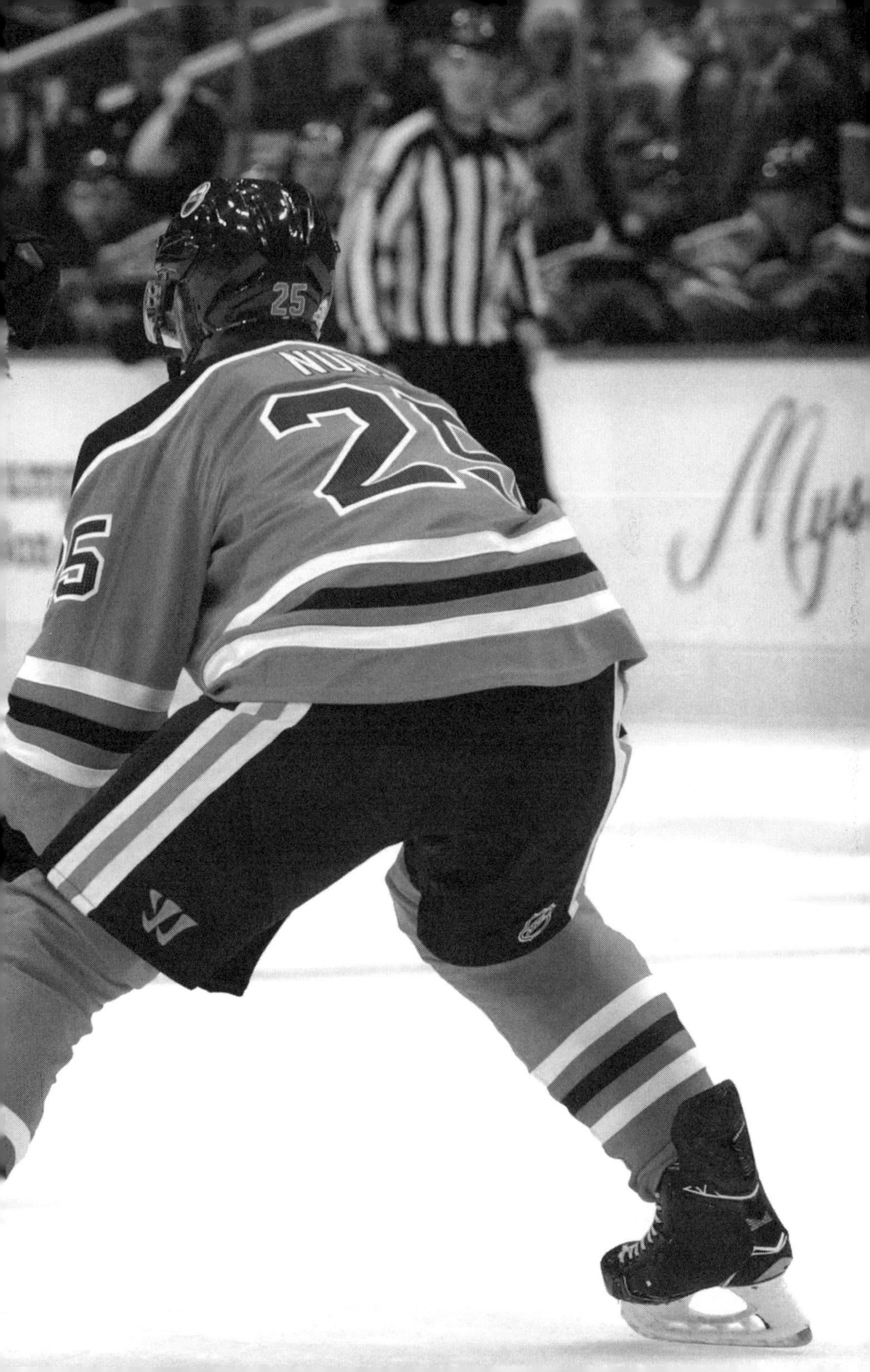
25

"The next three to five years, he'll be in the top two or three players in the game."

— Brad Crossley on Nathan MacKinnon

(Previous pages) Nathan MacKinnon takes a slapshot in front of Darnell Nurse of the Edmonton Oilers during an NHL game on Feb. 22, 2018, at Rogers Place in Edmonton.

CHAPTER 6
THE NATHAN MACKINNON STORY
The Next 'Next One'?

Nathan MacKinnon wasn't following in just anyone's footsteps. These were Sidney Crosby's footsteps – one of the best players of all time.

Yet while he doesn't have the three Stanley Cup rings or the scoring titles or the MVP trophies – yet – the "other" Cole Harbour hockey superstar has quickly developed into the NHL player everyone pegged him to be.

In fact, some see him ahead of his buddy Crosby when it comes to the best hockey players in the world today.

"He's Top 2 in the world. I think it's him and (Connor) McDavid. I would put Crosby at No. 3," says his former Halifax Mooseheads teammate Trey Lewis.

"The thing about Nathan is how competitive he is. He wants to win every single battle, every single race, even if it's practice. There were a couple of drills at practice (with the Mooseheads) that by the end of the year he refused to do because they would just get him so mad, so competitive. There were actually a couple scuffles with different players, but that's just how competitive he is."

MacKinnon played in the Cole Harbour minor hockey system and dominated from the beginning. In fact, it wasn't long before his name began making the rounds in local hockey circles as Nova Scotia's next big can't-miss prospect.

Nathan MacKinnon playing for Team Nova Scotia at the 2011 Canada Winter Games on February 13.

"He didn't want to be Sidney Crosby. But from a very young age, he wanted to do all of the things that Sidney Crosby did," Darren Cossar says. "At a very young age, he knew what he wanted to do – he wanted to play in the NHL and play at the highest level. But he was going to find his own way to do it and be his guy. The fact Sidney came from the same community really showed him if I do all the right things, if I have a plan, I can do it too."

FOCUS AND DETERMINATION

The numbers MacKinnon put up in minor hockey were astonishing. In atom, it's been reported that he had 200 points in 50 games played. By the time bantam AAA rolled around, he recorded more than 250 points over the course of two seasons.

"I remember talking to Darren Sutherland, our technical director for Hockey Nova Scotia, and he kept telling me the story of when (MacKinnon) was 13," Cossar says. "A little bit of a loner because he made sure he got the right amount of sleep, eating right, making

Nathan MacKinnon in action at the 2011 Canada Winter Games on February 13.

Nathan MacKinnon - Jan. 26th, 2011.

sure he was the first guy there for meetings, the first guy there on the ice. He was doing everything to make sure he had himself in the right spot, to achieve and succeed.

"To see that kind of focus on a 13-year-old that had skill ... there was absolutely no doubt Nathan was going to succeed at the next level, because he had a plan and he had that drive."

That meant following Crosby's path and playing at Shattuck-St. Mary's, spending two seasons at the Minnesota school. In Grade 9 while playing for its bantam tier 1 team, MacKinnon recorded 54 goals and 101 points. His Grade 10 season saw MacKinnon move up to boys under-16 and tally 45 goals and 93 points in 40 games.

With these numbers, it was no surprise MacKinnon was a sure-fire bet to go No. 1 overall in the Quebec Major Junior Hockey League draft. But after the Baie-Comeau Drakkar took him with the first pick, MacKinnon let it be known he wouldn't play for the northern Quebec-based club and threatened to return to Shattuck-St. Mary's. Eventually a deal was worked out to trade him to Halifax and play for his hometown Mooseheads.

"A lot of 16-year-olds who come into the league, they're sort of wide-eyed, maybe a little cautious, tentative," Lewis said. "That certainly wasn't the case with Nathan."

MacKinnon was a star in Halifax. He had 78 points in 58 games as a 16-year-old rookie, and then tallied 75 points in 44 games during his second year of junior. But where MacKinnon's star shone brightest was in the playoffs. He helped the Mooseheads make it to the league semifinals as a rookie and followed that up by leading a talent-laden Halifax club to its first and only QMJHL title in 2012-13.

MEMORIAL CUP STAR

MacKinnon kept that momentum going into that season's Memorial Cup in May 2013. In the championship final, he netted his second hat trick of the four-team tournament as Halifax defeated the Portland Winterhawks 6-4. MacKinnon was named Memorial Cup MVP and finished with seven goals and 13 points in four games as the Mooseheads completed their dream season.

"He did something a lot of people hoped for but weren't sure we'd ever win a Memorial Cup," Cossar said. "When you look at it realistically, that's a tough championship to win. To see a young man that determined and driven, it was special."

MacKinnon's handling of the pressure at the Memorial Cup showed he was ready for the NHL. The tournament was billed as a battle between two potential first-round NHL draft picks – MacKinnon and Seth Jones of the Winterhawks. Jones was ranked No. 1 by NHL Central Scouting for the draft, followed by MacKinnon at No. 2.

When all was said and done, it was MacKinnon who played the starring role and who iced the victory for the Mooseheads in the championship game. He scored his hat-trick goal into an empty net with only 22 seconds left in regulation time.

"I might not score a bigger goal in my life," MacKinnon was quoted as saying after the game in a Canadian Press story. "It's just ... 22 seconds left. We won it. We're champions. The empty netter will be in my mind forever."

MacKinnon has only fond memories of his time playing for the Mooseheads. He was given a hero's welcome at the 2019 Memorial Cup at the Scotiabank Centre in Halifax. He dropped the ceremonial faceoff for the championship game between Halifax and Rouyn-Noranda and was given a loud, lengthy standing ovation by the sold-out crowd.

"I grew up a huge Mooseheads fan. I billeted players. I have a very strong connection with this team," he told reporters before the championship game. "I was only here two years but it felt like a lot longer. I just finished my sixth in Colorado, but still with the

Darnell Nurse of the Edmonton Oilers chases Nathan MacKinnon during an NHL game on February 22, 2018 at Rogers Place in Edmonton.

Nathan MacKinnon speaks to reporters at the Memorial Cup at Scotiabank Centre in Halifax in May 2019.

Mooseheads, it felt like I was here for 10. I think the connection I have with the city is very strong. I come back every summer and train. All my family and friends live here. It's great."

Like Crosby eight years earlier, MacKinnon was taken first overall in the 2013 NHL draft, by the Colorado Avalanche. But unlike Crosby, MacKinnon captured the Calder Trophy as top NHL rookie after recording 24 goals and 63 points in 82 games. MacKinnon is the youngest player ever to win the trophy.

'EXPLOSIVE'

The next few years were less productive, as MacKinnon didn't surpass 53 points. But in the 2017-18 season, MacKinnon turned into the superstar everyone thought he would be. He ended the campaign with 39 goals and 97 points and finished second in voting for the Hart Trophy as NHL MVP. Then came his 99-point season in 2018-19, with a career-best 41 goals.

His 2019 playoffs were special to watch as well. He had eight points in five games as the Avalanche upended the top-seeded Calgary Flames in the first round. In Round 2, MacKinnon helped the Avalanche take the San Jose Sharks to a seventh and deciding game, which they ended up losing.

Nathan MacKinnon celebrates a Halifax Mooseheads goal on March 26, 2012.

MacKinnon played much of that Game 7 with a bad shoulder sprain after taking a hard hit to the boards. He almost scored in his first shift after suffering the injury, showing the character and will to win he possesses.

"I think he's in the top three to five players in the game right now," says Brad Crossley. "I thought this past year was a coming out year. He took control of his team. He's always been able to take control of his own talent, but he actually carried the team this year. His line did as well and I think that was a big thing for him."

When talking about what makes MacKinnon so special, everyone brings up his skating prowess. Crossley calls him the "most explosive player in the game right now."

"Nathan goes from 0 to 100 in split seconds," he said. "Just to watch him play the game at such a high speed level mesmerizes people. The only thing that matches that is his intensity level. He's maybe more intense than Sid at times on the ice."

Ken Reid calls MacKinnon the master of the straight crossovers. "I just love his foot speed," Reid said. "The way he handles the puck, he does it so quickly, plus his compete level. I think he's learned a lot from Sid – the compete level and the intensity he brings. And you can see as he gets older, I think he's getting more competitive. You could see the anger in his eyes when they lost out this year."

MacKinnon wants nothing more than to have his moment with the Stanley Cup some day. He's driven to win and the next few seasons will be interesting to watch as the Avalanche are building a strong nucleus around their superstar centre.

"He's really figuring out who he is. We got to see that this year, what he's capable of," Cossar says. "Knowing him as an individual, the determination and the drive, the plan he puts in place, I'd be shocked if he doesn't have a Stanley Cup before he is done."

'VERY PROUD TO BE FROM HERE'

Nathan MacKinnon knew he'd be hearing about it all summer long.

With both Sidney Crosby and Brad Marchand reaching 100 points, MacKinnon expected to get roasted about a 99-point season during off-season training.

"They both got 100 and I got 99. That's tough. Marchy's going to be all over me this summer at our skates," MacKinnon told reporters during the Memorial Cup in Halifax. "It's great. We're very proud to be from here. Brad has had such an amazing season and playoffs. Sid has won three Cups as well. We had good seasons, the three of us. It's cool to see fellow Maritimers do well."

The good news for MacKinnon is that he has plenty of time to get back at his two buddies. But this was a special season and one that may never get forgotten among the trio.

"He'll probably be getting chirped when he's 75 years old and they're all out golfing together at Ashburn," Ken Reid says.

CAREER NHL STATS

	GP	G	A	P
2013-14	82	24	39	63
2014-15	64	14	24	38
2015-16	72	21	31	52
2016-17	82	16	37	53
2017-18	74	39	58	97
2018-19	82	41	58	99
TOTALS	456	155	247	402

Source: NHL.com

Nathan MacKinnon holds the Memorial Cup after the Halifax Mooseheads defeated the Portland Winterhawks in the finals of the 2013 Memorial Cup in Saskatoon, on May 26, 2013. MacKinnon was named the tournament's MVP.

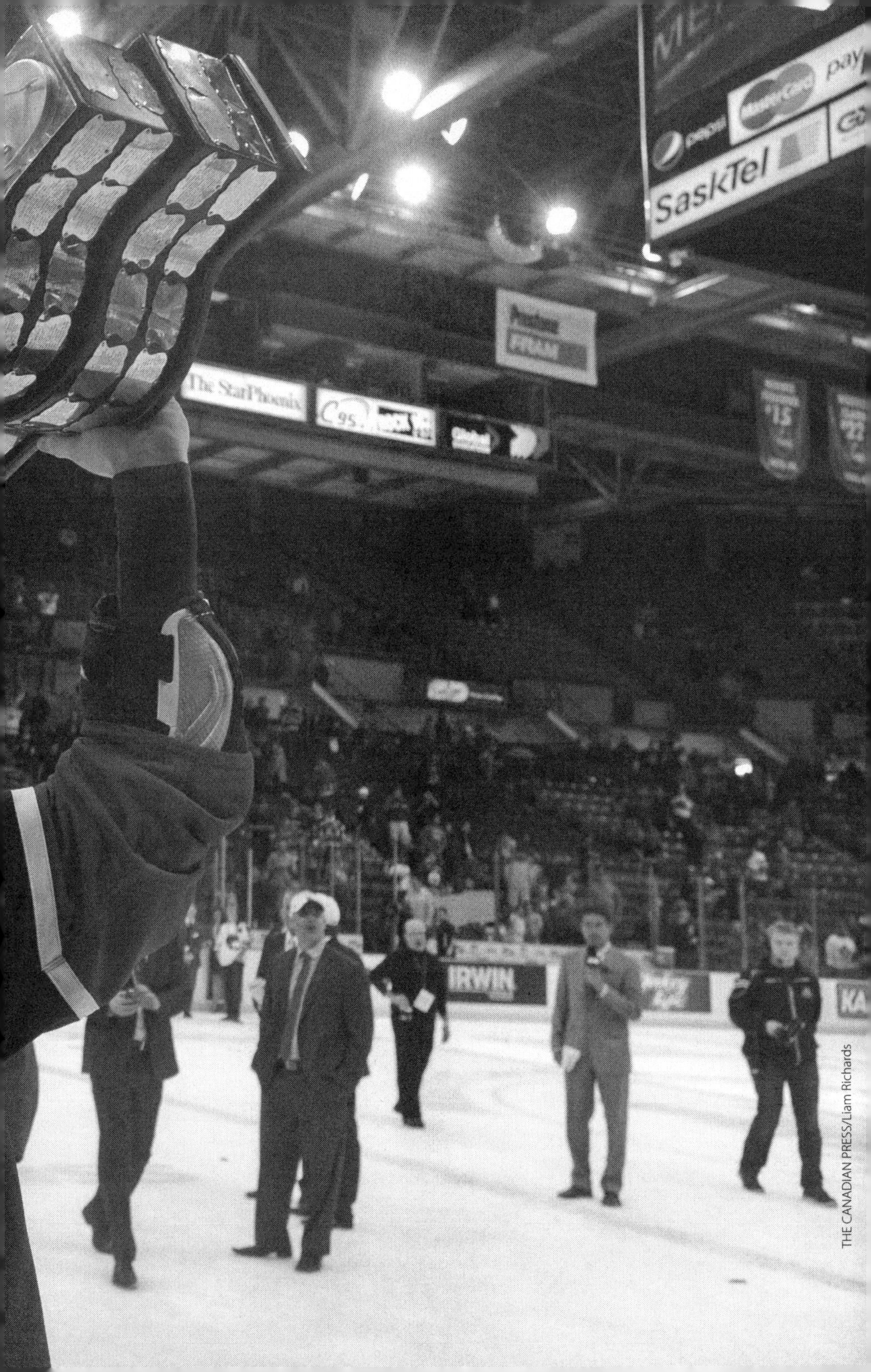

THE CANADIAN PRESS/Liam Richards

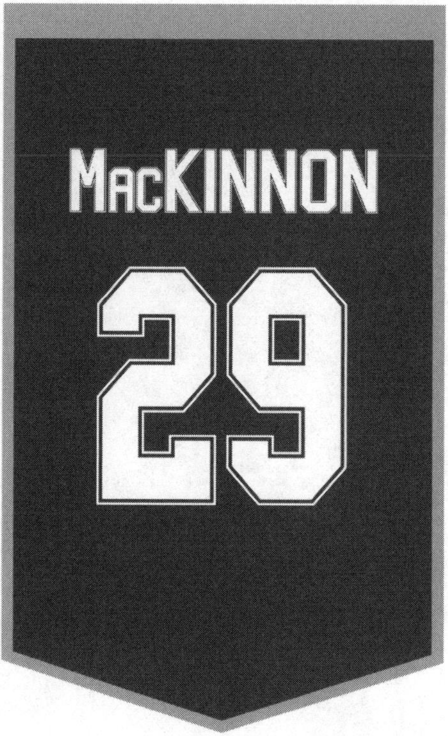
MacKINNON
29

CHAPTER 7
NATHAN MACKINNON'S SEASON

It's not a matter of if but when Nathan MacKinnon reaches the century mark for points in a regular season.

He turned 24 on Sept. 1 and is now entering his prime hockey years. As long as he can avoid serious injury, count on MacKinnon reaching 100 points more than a few times during his NHL career.
In 2018-19, there were a few blips on his offensive scorecard in the second half. The first half, he was simply on fire.

It came down to the wire for MacKinnon reaching 100 points and he finished just short.

Here's a month-by-month breakdown of how he reached 99.

OCTOBER – 18 points in 12 games

It was a great start to the season for MacKinnon.

He recorded points in nine straight games to begin the year and had three points in three separate games in the first month of play. That included three assists against the New Jersey Devils on Oct. 18, a goal and two assists Oct. 20 against the Carolina Hurricanes and then again Oct. 26 against the Ottawa Senators.

"(Our line), we've been playing well," MacKinnon told reporters after the team's 3-1 win in Carolina. "We had a decent first five or six games but not great, so I think the last two or three have been awesome. We're controlling the play a lot more. We just got some chances and took advantage."

OCTOBER	G	A	P	Shifts	Ice Time
4 – vs. Minnesota	1	0	1	22	22:32
6 – vs. Philadelphia	1	1	2	24	23:55
9 – at Columbus	1	0	1	24	20:46
11 – at Buffalo	2	0	2	19	19:20
13 – vs. Calgary	1	0	1	27	22:25
16 – at N.Y. Rangers	1	0	1	27	22:33
18 – at New Jersey	0	3	3	23	21:42
20 – at Carolina	1	2	3	24	20:58
22 – at Philadelphia	0	1	1	23	19:51
24 – vs. Tampa Bay	0	0	0	24	22:45
26 – vs. Ottawa	1	2	3	26	23:48
27 – at Minnesota	0	0	0	24	24:24
Source: NHL.com					

NOVEMBER – 23 points in 14 games

Another great month for MacKinnon that put him ahead of the scoring pace needed to reach 100 points through about a third of the season.

He had nine multiple-point games for the month, including two goals and an assist against the Vancouver Canucks on Nov. 2 and a goal and three assists against Crosby and the Penguins on Nov. 28. "I'm sure this will be a game we talk about for a while," MacKinnon told reporters that night.

Crosby had a hat trick on the way to a 6-3 win for Colorado. "We don't play each other much. For regular season games, this is one of the more fun ones I've been a part of."

The four-point game capped a stretch where MacKinnon recorded six goals and nine assists in six games.

NOVEMBER	G	A	P	Shifts	Ice Time
1 – at Calgary	0	0	0	25	23:18
2 – at Vancouver	2	1	3	28	23:56
7 – vs. Nashville	0	1	1	26	24:28
9 – at Winnipeg	0	0	0	24	23:21
11 – at Edmonton	0	2	2	21	18:52
14 – vs. Boston	1	1	2	23	22:08
16 – vs. Washington	0	0	0	25	21:55
18 – at Anaheim	1	2	3	29	25:43
21 – at Los Angeles	1	1	2	20	18:12
23 – at Arizona	0	2	2	21	19:32
24 – vs. Dallas	1	1	2	24	22:23
27 – at Nashville	2	0	2	23	21:24
28 – vs. Pittsburgh	1	3	4	27	20:55
30 – vs. St. Louis	0	0	0	26	22:57
Source: NHL.com					

DECEMBER	G	A	P	Shifts	Ice Time
2 – at Detroit	1	1	2	23	21:11
4 – at Pittsburgh	0	0	0	25	21:52
6 – at Florida	0	1	1	22	19:26
8 – at Tampa Bay	1	0	1	20	19:38
11 – vs. Edmonton	0	2	2	23	23:41
14 – at St. Louis	0	1	1	26	25:47
15 – vs. Dallas	1	3	4	24	19:58
17 – vs. N.Y. Islanders	0	1	1	26	22:23
19 – vs. Montreal	0	2	2	24	20:54
21 – vs. Chicago	0	0	0	23	22:55
22 – at Arizona	1	0	1	25	21:51
27 – at Vegas	0	1	1	26	23:15
29 – vs. Chicago	1	0	1	25	23:43
31 – vs. Los Angeles	1	0	1	27	21:53

Source: NHL.com

DECEMBER – 18 points in 14 games

MacKinnon kept rolling offensively in December.

While not as productive as the previous months, he still had four multiple-point games, including a goal and three assists against the Dallas Stars on Dec. 15.

It was MacKinnon's second four-point game of the season. When December ended, MacKinnon stood at 59 points through 40 games. In comparison, Marchand had 41 points when December wrapped up. Crosby was at 48.

JANUARY – 12 points in 10 games

It was an average month offensively for MacKinnon.

He had another four multiple-point games, including a goal and two assists against the New York Rangers on Jan. 4.

Unfortunately, MacKinnon's most memorable play of the month happened on the bench in a game against the Flames in Calgary on Jan. 9: getting into a shouting match with Avalanche head coach Jared Bednar late in a 5-3 loss.

The clip of an angry MacKinnon made headlines across North America and it showed him throwing a water bottle and falling backwards off the bench in frustration.

"That's unacceptable on my part," MacKinnon told media in Montreal on Jan. 11. "I can't be doing that stuff. It was just frustrating as we have lost eight of nine. I think Tkachuk just scored an empty netter and I was just really frustrated. But I love playing for Bedsy. Everyone loves playing for Bedsy in here. That's on me and I take responsibility for it."

JANUARY	G	A	P	Shifts	Ice Time
2 – vs. San Jose	0	1	1	28	23:19
4 – vs. N.Y. Rangers	1	2	3	20	21:09
8 – at Winnipeg	0	2	2	24	22:20
9 – at Calgary	1	0	1	25	25:37
12 – at Montreal	0	0	0	24	24:08
14 – at Toronto	0	0	0	24	21:15
16 – at Ottawa	1	1	2	21	23:48
19 – vs. Los Angeles	0	2	2	18	14:52
21 – vs. Nashville	0	0	0	23	21:06
23 – vs. Minnesota	0	1	1	21	18:39
Source: NHL.com					

FEBRUARY – 10 points in 14 games

It was a tough month for MacKinnon, taking him off pace in his bid for 100 points.

He had six scoreless games in February and had only one multiple-point game, on Feb. 23, with two goals and an assist against the Nashville Predators.

MacKinnon stood at 81 points when February ended with 18 games left.

FEBRUARY	G	A	P	Shifts	Ice Time
2 – vs. Vancouver	0	0	0	25	21:45
5 – vs. Columbus	0	1	1	26	21:52
7 – at Washington	1	0	1	26	23:29
9 – at N.Y. Islanders	0	0	0	26	19:30
10 – at Boston	1	0	1	29	22:44
12 – vs. Toronto	0	0	0	24	19:50
14 – at Winnipeg	0	1	1	24	20:43
16 – vs. St. Louis	0	0	0	24	20:17
18 – vs. Vegas	0	1	1	23	19:33
20 – vs. Winnipeg	1	0	1	26	22:14
22 – at Chicago	0	0	0	26	22:02
23 – at Nashville	2	1	3	23	19:53
25 – vs. Florida	0	0	0	27	21:56
27 – vs. Vancouver	1	0	1	27	23:29

Source: NHL.com

MARCH	G	A	P	Shifts	Ice Time
1 – vs. San Jose	0	1	1	27	23:24
3 – at Anaheim	0	0	0	24	24:11
5 – vs. Detroit	1	1	2	29	24:35
7 – at Dallas	0	0	0	22	23:53
9 – vs. Buffalo	1	2	3	26	22:23
11 – vs Carolina	0	0	0	27	21:54
15 – vs. Anaheim	1	1	2	27	22:32
17 – vs. New Jersey	1	1	2	25	22:02
19 – at Minnesota	0	0	0	31	23:37
21 – at Dallas	0	0	0	27	23:13
23 – vs. Chicago	0	0	0	27	24:02
24 – at Chicago	0	1	1	29	23:56
27 – vs. Las Vegas	1	1	2	27	21:18
29 – vs. Arizona	1	0	1	29	21:47
Source: NHL.com					

MARCH – 14 points in 14 games

MacKinnon got back to a point-per-game pace in March but still didn't have many standout games offensively.

He finished with five multiple-point games, the highest being a three-point effort against the Buffalo Sabres on March 9. He had six games where he didn't score a point, including three consecutive contests – March 19 against Minnesota, March 21 against Dallas and March 23 against Chicago.

Going into the month of April, MacKinnon stood at 95 points with four games left in the regular season.

APRIL – 4 points in 4 games

MacKinnon kept up his point-per-game pace with an assist April 1 against St. Louis, then potted his 40th goal of the season April 2 against the Edmonton Oilers. He also had one helper against the Winnipeg Jets on April 4.

Sitting at 98 points and playing the San Jose Sharks on the final day of the regular season, MacKinnon hit point 99 when he scored two minutes into the second period. But the Avalanche were shut out for the remainder of the game, with MacKinnon unable to reach 100 points despite playing more than 24 minutes and firing five shots on goal.

The team would pull its goalie with about 4 minutes remaining to try to get MacKinnon to the century mark, but it was to no avail.

"He probably played three and a half minutes of the last four with an empty net (and on) the power plays," MacKinnon's head coach Jared Bednar was quoted on avalanche.com. "I think that is why the 6 versus 5 probably wasn't as effective as it could have been because everyone wanted to get it over to Nate so he could touch it before we made something happen, and he was pushing it. I think at that point in the game, the game is on the line but it's two goals, it is the last couple minutes. I would love to see him get 100 too but just didn't happen."

APRIL	G	A	P	Shifts	Ice Time
1 – at St. Louis	0	1	1	26	21:33
2 – vs. Edmonton	1	0	1	21	18:09
4 – vs. Winnipeg	0	1	1	27	26:41
6 – at San Jose	1	0	1	21	24:20
Source: NHL.com					

Nathan MacKinnon of the Colorado Avalanche during a game on December 18, 2016 at the MTS Centre in Winnipeg.

Rusty Barton/Hockey Hall of Fame

Rusty Barton/Hockey Hall of Fame

(Top Left) Brad Marchand during a game on March 14, 2019 at Bell MTS Place in Winnipeg.

(Left) Sidney Crosby ties his skates during a warmup before a game on October 29, 2017 at Bell MTS Place in Winnipeg.

(Top Right) Nathan MacKinnon and Connor Hellebuyck of the Winnipeg Jets during a game on March 4, 2017 at MTS Centre in Winnipeg.

Rusty Barton/Hockey Hall of Fame

"I really liked what I learned that day. Andy knew what he was doing getting around the gym. I kind of asked him if he would ever be interested in doing some sessions."

— Sidney Crosby in a 2015 Sportsnet story on how his relationship with trainer Andy O'Brien began.

CHAPTER 8
TRAINING TOGETHER

They're practices you could easily sell tickets to. Sidney Crosby, Nathan MacKinnon and Brad Marchand, three of the biggest names in hockey, sharing the same ice each summer to get ready for the upcoming NHL season.

John Moore has been allowed to record video of these closed practices at the BMO Centre in Bedford the past six summers for his website Sports and Moore. His clips are posted to his YouTube channel and regularly picked up by the likes of TSN and Sportsnet and shown to hockey fans across North America.

One of the most watched videos from the summer of 2019 was a string of puck battles between Crosby and MacKinnon. The intensity displayed in the three-minute video is what you'd expect to see during an NHL game, but it highlights the work this trio puts in each summer to get themselves ready for the upcoming season.

"Honestly, I can sit and watch them all day long," Moore says. "It's a practice, but they bring a compete level that is almost like game on. The drills that they do are all up-tempo. Everything is simulated to games, one-on-one battles, lots of skating and battling.

Nathan MacKinnon and the rest of Team Canada get ready to take on Team Slovakia in preliminary round action at the 2013 IIHF Ice Hockey U20 World Championship.

"You can see the pride in their game and how they hold themselves to a high standard. You can't help but notice the intensity during the practices. I could stand there all day and watch it."

The on-ice sessions are by invitation only and can feature two or three goalies, five or six defencemen and eight or nine forwards.

Most of those joining Crosby, MacKinnon and Marchand are either NHLers from Nova Scotia, or those who are playing professionally, whether it be the American Hockey League, East Coast Hockey League, or in Europe. There are also sometimes players from university or even junior.

"If you are a young prospect in the American Hockey League or hoping to get an invite to an NHL camp, you want to not disappoint anybody and you want to get invited back," Moore says.

"You don't want to embarrass yourself. I feel for the goaltenders. There is a group of them out there … some local guys who go to Europe …. and they get shelled. You have guys that are usually good pro goalies who are playing in, say, the American Hockey

League, or university all-stars like Chase Marchand, all-Canadians, and they're getting lit up."

But sometimes even other NHLers from outside Nova Scotia will drop by.

In 2014, then-Avalanche forward Matt Duchene joined Crosby and Co. on the ice. This summer, it was the top pick of the 2019 draft, Jack Hughes of the New Jersey Devils, who travelled to Halifax to don the blades.

"Wouldn't you want to be part of it? I know there are certain guys around town not invited to it for whatever reason," Moore says. "It's an exclusive group. It's pretty cool."

Brad Crossley, Crosby's friend and former coach with the Dartmouth Subways of the Nova Scotia Major Midget Hockey League, has been on the ice with No. 87 for about 15 consecutive summers with the job of helping him get ready for the upcoming hockey season.

Crossley says the length of off-season training for NHL players can depend on how long they go into the post-season, but it's not long before they're into it. It starts off the ice and then develops into both on- and off-ice workouts.

"Some of the guys, like Sid has had extended seasons the last number of years, so he may need a little more time off just to recover, re-energize, clear his mind mentally," Crossley says. "But normally they start and are fully into it in June with their off-ice programs intensely at three to five days a week."

SUMMER TRAINING IN HALIFAX AND COLORADO

July is when the on-ice practices start up again. Crossley says the 90-or-so-minute sessions usually begin around Canada Day and go two to three days a week. When August hits, it goes to three to five days a week.

Crosby and MacKinnon are on the ice most days. Marchand is in and out a bit more because of his family life in Boston, but when he's in town, he's there.

"Sid will call me in the summer and say, 'Listen, I'm not ready for you yet. I have to get on the ice a few more times before you come out,'" Crossley says chuckling. "He and I have a great relationship that way, to the point where now I get to go to Vail, Colorado with 23 of the best guys in the NHL and run a five-day camp for them."

"But it's all because of Sid and the relationship we have."

The camp Crossley refers to in Colorado is run by Andy O'Brien, who has become a trainer to the stars in the world of sports. His list of clients includes Crosby, MacKinnon, women's hockey star Hayley Wickenheiser and figure skating legend Patrick Chan.

O'Brien, who is from Charlottetown and is a sports performance specialist, first met Crosby in the summer of 2000 while the 13-year-old phenom was attending a hockey camp in Canada's smallest province. Crosby liked O'Brien's off-ice workouts so much that by next summer the two began daily training sessions in Halifax.

They've been at it every summer since.

"The early days were pretty long, from what I remember," Crosby said about O'Brien in a story posted on Sportsnet.ca in 2016.

"We'd have a track workout, then we'd go in the gym, then we'd go do something at (Citadel) Hill. It didn't really feel necessarily like we were working out."

PUTTING IN THE WORK PAYS OFF

O'Brien's relationship to the hockey superstar is so strong that in 2015 the Penguins hired him as director of sport science and performance. Pittsburgh and Crosby have gone on to win two Stanley Cups since that hiring, with No. 87 giving credit to O'Brien for playing as well as he did.

"It's really hard to believe it's been that long," Crosby told Sportsnet.ca about his nearly two-decade relationship with O'Brien. "Going through different injuries, and what he's been there for, it meant a lot. I know how badly he wanted to win the Stanley Cup, so it was nice to be able to share that with him."

Jeff Petry of the Montreal Canadiens stickhandles in front of Brad Marchand during a game on November 24, 2018 at the Bell Centre in Montreal. The Bruins beat the Canadiens 3-2.

"Sidney and I are both equally ambitious. We're constantly talking about his success and results," O'Brien said in a 2015 Sportsnet story about their relationship.

"That being said, I probably care more about him as a person than as an athlete. I have as much interest in his overall happiness than I do in his performance."

MacKinnon is also close to O'Brien and spends part of his summers training with him. They began working together after his first year at Shattuck-St. Mary's and MacKinnon's improved fitness has helped to develop him into the player he is today.

"The mentality to put in the work, willingness and intensity, was there right away, like it was with Sid," O'Brien said in a 2018 Sportsnet story" on MacKinnon and his No. 5 ranking in the NHL's Top 100 players list for the 2018-19 season.

"I never had to motivate Nate. I just give him the structure and the details and he became a student of it. He wanted to understand everything he could to become a better player."

That includes joining Crosby and other elite NHLers that O'Brien trains – including Toronto Maple Leafs forward John Tavares and New Jersey Devils star Taylor Hall – for a five-day, late-summer intensive camp in Vail, Colorado.

Crossley runs the on-ice sessions in Vail, with O'Brien mapping out the day's schedules and workouts. Crossley says the players are ready to take their training to another level when they get to Vail with NHL training camps around the corner.

"We're two days into the camp (one year) and Sidney meets me at the side and says, 'You know, Cros, we have to go harder. This just isn't hard enough,'" Crossley says when discussing how the intensity picks up. "Sid's out there and he wants to test the guys as competitors and see what they have as well.

"So the next couple of practices some of the guys were coming up to me and saying, 'I heard Sid talked to you about going harder.' And they're huffing and puffing. There are a handful of guys at Sid's level in their work ethic, Nathan being one of them. John Tavares, guys like that. Sid's got a work ethic second to none and a lot of guys are inspired and driven by that."

Marchand has a different off-season trainer. J.P. MacCallum is a former player with the Saint Mary's Huskies who is now a strength and conditioning coach. MacCallum began training Marchand when he was a 13-year-old bantam AAA player and they have been together ever since.

In fact, MacCallum was one of several people Marchand thanked publicly in 2011 when the Bruins won the Stanley Cup and the Boston forward brought the trophy back to Halifax.

"It's certainly been a wild ride with Brad," MacCallum told theScore in a 2019 story about Marchand's development as a player.

"It's been 17 years now, 17 off-seasons that we've worked together. So starting with when he was a 13-year-old, at the bantam level in Nova Scotia. He always had the competitive spirit. ... You saw the competitive factor, he was a good player, but there was nobody that would've said at the time that he was going to play in the NHL."

The story talks about the workout plan MacCallum and Marchand have developed over the years. Their primary focus is on strengthening his legs to help combat his smaller size when battling for pucks in the corners.

"I think in hockey if you look at a lot of the guys, their body makeup, a lot of them have very big lower bodies," Marchand says in the story. "That's a focus nowadays. Before, I think a lot of guys worried about their strength and getting big and strong, but the game, the way it is now, it's all speed and endurance and skill, so you know it's pretty much all legs."

With the amount of work this trio is putting into off-season workouts, it's not hard to see why they're doing so well when matched with their amazing skill level. It also shows why none of them appears to be slowing down, especially Crosby and Marchand who are now in their 30s.

"I see them get better and better and better over the course of time," Moore says. "But they work so hard at it I'm not surprised. It's the summer and that's when the work boots go on and they go at it."

'THE PLAYERS, THEY LIKE BRAD'

While arguably the most hated man in hockey, Brad Marchand has plenty of friends for on-ice training.

John Moore says while Sidney Crosby and Nathan MacKinnon are best buddies off the ice, it's clear the Cole Harbour duo enjoys Marchand's company during their on-ice summer training.

In fact, Marchand can get smiles out of everyone through his laidback demeanour.

"He is a liked guy. The general public likes to make him Public Enemy No. 1, but the players, they like Brad. He's a funny guy," Moore says. "He's got a sense of humour. I'm out there and he makes me laugh. He really does."

During line drills, Marchand, Crosby and MacKinnon will often be found skating together. And when things don't go the way they think it should, the mood can quickly change.

"You can see when they don't complete that perfect three-way passing play, you can see the frustration. 'Why can't we do that?'" Moore says. "They believe they should do that every time they come up the ice. They have a high standard."

Ryan Taplin photo

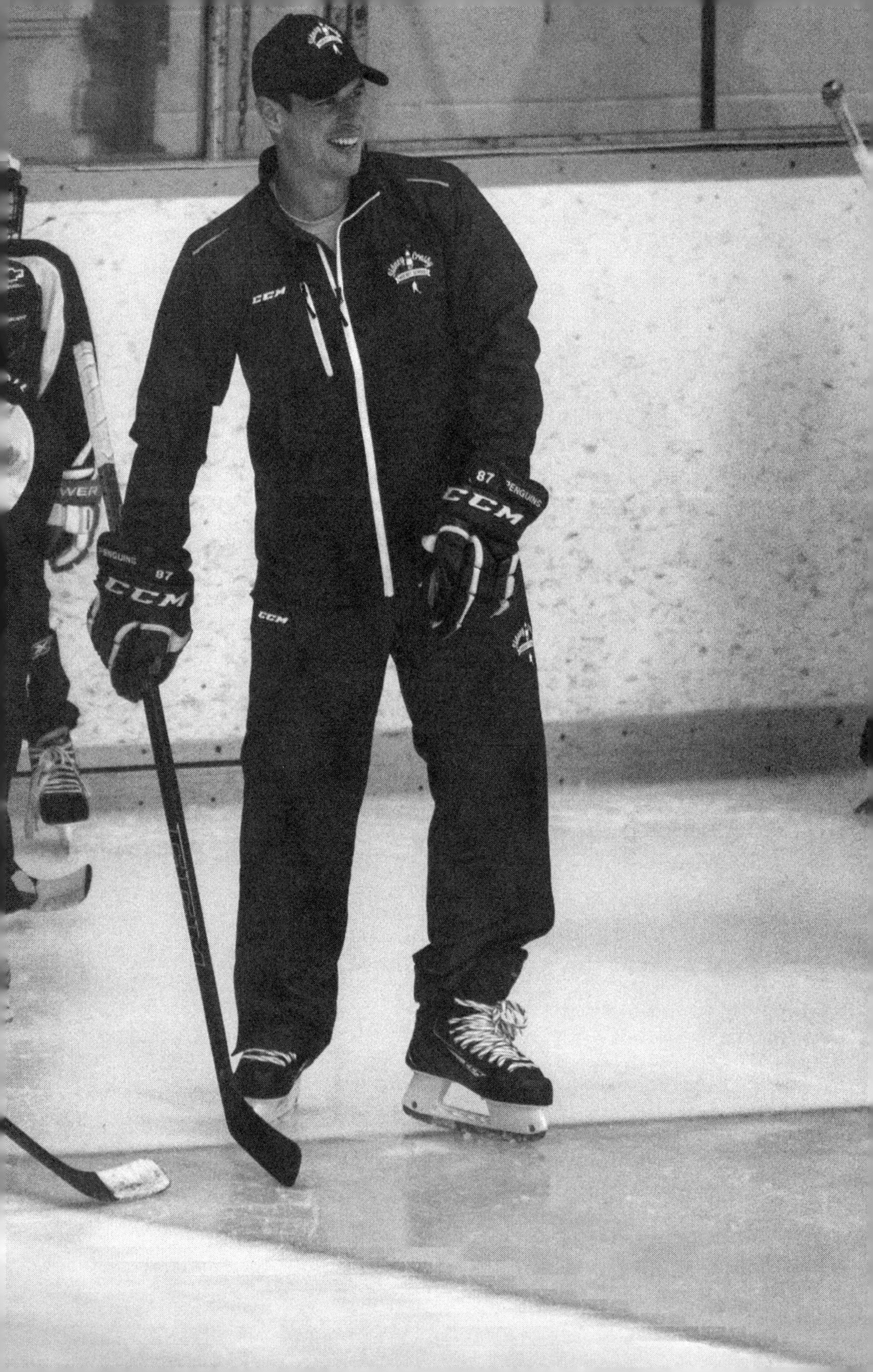
CCM
87
PENGUINS
CCM
PENGUINS
87
CCM
CCM

"People from my hometown have always made it a point to give back. I always told myself that if I ever get to this point, I would do the same. I think a lot of guys have the same approach. You feel lucky to do what you do. If you can help out in other ways, and this puts you in that position, you try to do your best."

— Sidney Crosby in an interview with the Pittsburgh Post-Gazette's Jason Mackey in 2017

(Previous pages) Sidney Crosby chats with some of the kids at his second annual hockey school at Cole Harbour Place on July 11, 2016.

CHAPTER 9
GIVING BACK

It's the little things sometimes that can have the biggest impact.

Matthew Stienburg of Halifax was only 15 when he suddenly received a text from NHL star Brad Marchand. He had just completed one of two surgeries required for osteomyelitis, an infection in his shoulder which was eating at his muscle and bones. The diagnosis came as he was playing bantam AAA hockey and was developing into an elite hockey prospect in Nova Scotia.

After one of his two surgeries, Marchand checked in from Boston to see how the talented forward was doing. Stienburg was blown away.

"To be 15 years old and to be getting a text from an NHL player that you weren't really expecting, it's a little thing that goes a long way," says Stienburg, taken in the third round by the Colorado Avalanche in the 2019 NHL draft. "It gives you the extra motivation to keep going."

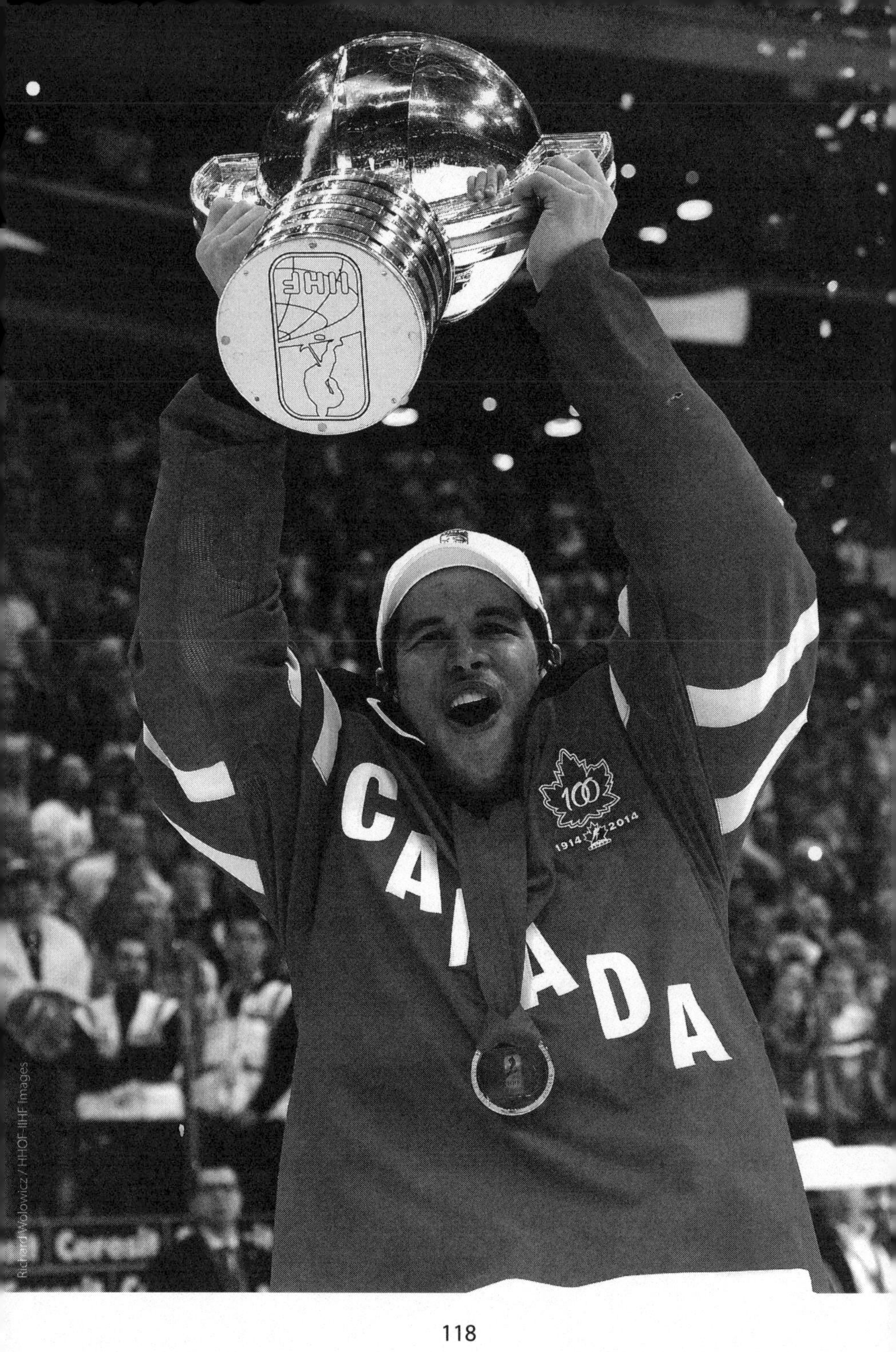

Richard Wolowicz / HHOF-IIHF Images

As great as Marchand, Crosby and MacKinnon are on the ice, they are just as great off of it for giving back and being receptive to fans in their home city and province.

Sometimes, stories about the good deeds they do make headlines in Nova Scotia and across North America.

A recent example came in the summer of 2018 when Crosby donated $50,000 to Special Olympics Nova Scotia through the Sidney Crosby Foundation before the national games that year in Antigonish, Nova Scotia.

Three years earlier when Crosby and MacKinnon played for Canada at the IIHF World Men's Hockey Championship, they donated their salaries from the tournament to the Cole Harbour Minor Hockey Association. According to an article in The Hockey News on Aug. 6, 2015, Team Canada earned 1 million Swiss Francs for winning all their games in regulation time and the money was then split between the players.

"Obviously this is where Nate and I started so to have the opportunity to give back and ... to be able to have it go directly to the minor hockey associations that we were a part of means a lot to us," Crosby is quoted as saying to The Chronicle Herald. "I'm sure it'll go a long way."

(Opposite) Canada's Sidney Crosby lifts the championship trophy after a 6-1 win over Team Russia in the gold medal game at the 2015 IIHF Ice Hockey World Championship.

'NO SPEECHES. NO FANFARE'

Marchand is giving back in many ways too. One example came in the summer of 2015 at the Maritime NHLers for Kids golf tournament at Digby Pines.

Tricia Titus, a single mother of four hockey-playing boys, was at the event with her kids as guests of Maritime NHLers For Kids, which helps to ease the financial costs of hockey for young people in Nova Scotia, New Brunswick and Prince Edward Island.

According to a story by The Digby Courier, Marchand won an auction bid through Enterprise Car Rental for two tickets to the 2016 NHL all-star game in Nashville.

Before winning the bid, the story says Marchand made the company bump the prize up to five tickets.

He then went on stage and announced he would be paying for the flights and hotel for Titus's whole family to go to the all-star weekend, together.

"After that I don't remember much," Titus says in a 2016 article. "I was bawling, my sister was crying, my friends were crying."

Long-time hockey broadcaster John Moore has heard countless stories of how this trio gives back. He's even seen it with his own eyes.

"I've witnessed it so often. They don't do it just when the media is there, when the spotlight is on them or there is a camera rolling. They do it when no one is watching," Moore says.

"They don't go looking for attention. They don't want to draw attention to themselves."

An example Moore gives is about Marchand and the Jordan Boyd Foundation.

Nathan MacKinnon of the Halifax Mooseheads celebrates following a goal on January 26, 2011.

Boyd, a 16-year-old from Bedford, was attending a training camp for the Quebec Major Junior Hockey League's Acadie-Bathurst Titan when, with his parents watching from the stands, he collapsed on the ice on Aug. 12, 2013.

Despite efforts from paramedics, Boyd died in hospital soon after. They later learned that Boyd had an undiagnosed and inherited heart condition called arrhythmogenic right ventricular cardiomyopathy.

Since then, a celebrity hockey challenge has been held each summer to raise money for the Jordan Boyd Foundation, which is helping raise awareness of inherited heart diseases in young people, notably athletes.

Moore remembers watching Marchand those first few years at the event and was impressed with the work he was putting in to make sure it succeeded.

"He spent hours upon hours upon hours at the rink when he could have left the rink out the back door," Moore says. "But he was on the ice, talking to the media, doing whatever he could, to help get the Jordan Boyd foundation off its feet. Not wanting anything in return."

A similar type of story happened in 2011 when Crosby visited patients at the IWK Health Centre in Halifax, as it celebrated the grand opening of a new teen lounge, made possible with a donation from the Sidney Crosby Foundation. The IWK serves women and children from Nova Scotia, New Brunswick and Prince Edward Island.

"Sidney wanted to experience what a typical day is like inside the newly renovated teen lounge. No speeches. No fanfare," according to Trena Crewe, senior director of philanthropy and donor strategy for the IWK Foundation, in a blog post after the grand opening.

"What impressed me the most was just how comfortable Sidney was with everyone. He played pool, tried his hand at crafts … and jammed out to Rock Band. He laughed with some patients, talked quietly with others and made each and every youth feel special."

Sidney Crosby and his family do a lot of giving back through the foundation, which lists Crosby and his parents among its trustees and had more than $1 million in assets in the 2018 fiscal year. The foundation has built a new gym for Churchill Academy, a school in Dartmouth, Nova Scotia, that caters to kids with special educational needs, in addition to the donations to the IWK Health Centre's teen lounge, and to Special Olympics Nova Scotia.

There are also countless stories on social media of how the trio stop what they're doing wherever they may be in Halifax and sign autographs and take photos with fans.

It shouldn't be forgotten that after Crosby's three Stanley Cup triumphs and Marchand's one, the most famous trophy in sports was brought back each time to the Halifax region for parades, trips to hospitals, you name it. It was part of them saying thank you to fans and the community.

So why do Marchand, MacKinnon and Crosby love to come back home each summer? It's because their individual space is respected so well. And while giving back is important, so is having time to relax with family and friends.

This isn't lost on Moore.

"We give them their private time, which they need," he says. "They have homes on quiet lakes and they can escape to privacy there, and have their family lives.

"They come back to Nova Scotia each summer and they can't wait to come back, so they obviously love Nova Scotia and the community here."

"Fans understand how special these players are and how fortunate we are to have them. In this province, in this community, . . . it's had an impact on the hockey community, the dreams of young minor players. It is possible. I can play in the National Hockey League. The dream is very much alive in the minor hockey community as a result of those three players."

— John Moore of Sports and Moore on the impact of Sidney Crosby, Nathan MacKinnon and Brad Marchand

CHAPTER 10
THEIR LEGACY

They have become the faces of hockey in Nova Scotia and rightfully so.

Sidney Crosby has been carrying the mantle for more than a decade but now has some solid company in Nathan MacKinnon and Brad Marchand.

The impact these three have had on Nova Scotia hockey will be felt for years to come.

If you have the talent, and you put in the work, you too can make it and be like them. There are no guarantees, but they are giving young players hope and someone to idolize.

"I grew up in the '80s and the Oilers were on another planet," Jody Shelley says when talking about the impact Crosby, Marchand and MacKinnon can have on young hockey players in Nova Scotia.

"These guys have heroes in their hometowns. There are heroes in Halifax – it's so important for these young kids to realize that local kids are making it, or they can go to Cole Harbour and Dartmouth and watch them practise.

"It's tremendous what it does for the young kids."

It's not just in Nova Scotia. Go to home games in Pittsburgh, Colorado or Boston, and their jerseys are everywhere. Even for road games, fans show up wearing their names and team colours.

"Those three and the impact they are having on the game nationally and internationally, everyone wants to be like them. It says a lot," says Brad Crossley. "They're leading in the right ways."

Nathan MacKinnon playing for Team Nova Scotia at the 2011 Canada Winter Games on February 13.

Ryan Taplin photo

'YOU HAVE TO LOVE IT'

In 2018, Crosby was voted the No. 1 athlete in the province's history by the Nova Scotia Sport Hall of Fame. The Top 15 list, which also included Port Hood's Al MacInnis at No. 3, saw Crosby take centre stage at the Halifax Convention Centre.

"I don't really think about it as much as I think about what they mean to me," Crosby said when hall CEO Bruce Rainnie asked him about what he means to Nova Scoita. "I'm certainly proud to call this my home and I love coming back every summer. You feel the support everywhere."

Crosby was also asked what kids can learn from his story.

"I think the biggest thing from me when I think about it is passion. Passion is what is going to drive you to have success, passion is what is going to push you through obstacles and it's that passion that is going to push you to learn and grow.

"You have to love it. That's the way I see it."

Right now, Nova Scotia "punches outside of its weight class" when it comes to producing top-level NHL players, according to Darren Cossar. Even within Atlantic Canada over the past two decades, New Brunswick, Newfoundland and Labrador, and Prince Edward Island haven't been able to produce the quality of stars that Nova Scotia has.

"To put my finger on it, I'm not sure there's a single thing," Cossar says about why Nova Scotia is standing out among the four Atlantic provinces.

"The thing that jumps out to me is (Hockey Nova Scotia) built a high-performance program that really set the path for those players to move along. They mirrored it after Hockey Canada's program, so that those kids, it wasn't a big shock as they moved to the next level. But it also instilled in them what it would take to get there."

Liam MacDonald dives to knock the puck away from Sidney Crosby, at Crosby's hockey school at Cole Harbour Place on July 11, 2016.

EXTRA MOTIVATION

One of those players hoping to 'get there' is Halifax's Matthew Stienburg, whose father Trevor is a former NHLer and the long-time Saint Mary's Huskies men's hockey coach.

Stienburg was drafted in the third round, 63rd overall, by the Colorado Avalanche in 2019. The first of several Nova Scotians taken at the June draft in Vancouver, the former major midget star with the Halifax McDonald's has committed to play NCAA Division 1 hockey next season at Cornell University and wants to complete his degree before turning professional.

"Seeing those guys who have gone through the same rinks as us and played under the same coaches, it gives you a little bit of extra motivation, to know that it is possible," the 18-year-old says about the impact Crosby, MacKinnon and Marchand are having on the next generation.

"I think that's the biggest thing. It doesn't mean you're out (and can't make it) if you're not playing in some other places in the bigger cities."

Stienburg can't help but think about one day sharing the ice with these Halifax-area superstars. He said he now knows MacKinnon and Crosby well enough to say hello and has built a growing friendship with Marchand through Brad's younger brother and former Huskies forward Jeff Marchand.

"It's special to have that connection," he says. "You take a lot of pride from where you are from. To share that with a smaller group of guys, it's something that is pretty special."

Trevor Stienburg says it means the world to players like his son and others who get drafted or hope to be drafted one day into the NHL from Nova Scotia to see Crosby, MacKinnon and Marchand excelling like they are.

"The skill, talent and character has always been down here, but with the Quebec league opening up … they see it right in front of him on how to make it to the next step," says the proud father, himself taken by the Quebec Nordiques in the first round, 15th overall, in the 1984 NHL draft.

"Sid, Nate and Brad, they are all best in the world, so you now feel there's hope there. You look at them and you go, 'They put their pants on one leg at a time. They're right there. I can watch them and they're good guys.'

"It just becomes a little bit more attainable or guys feel that if I really push, maybe the same thing can happen to them."

Now, it's time to see what Crosby, MacKinnon and Marchand have in store for the 2019-20 season. The trio will be gunning again for 100 points as they try to lead their respective teams back to the playoffs.

It would be great to see them all get to the century mark together in one season, but it's a big ask. The 2018-19 season was something very special.

"I see it as really difficult (to match or beat what they did)," Cossar says. "I would never say never, but boy, that's tough to top."

THREE ALL STARS ALL TOGETHER

If Sidney Crosby, Nathan MacKinnon and Brad Marchand chasing 100 points in a regular season wasn't enough of a legacy for Nova Scotia hockey, consider that these three were also named to the NHL all-star game in 2018. A photo of the three was taken to capture the moment with Crosby in the middle, Marchand on his left and MacKinnon to his right.

There was also the 2016 World Cup of Hockey, which included Crosby and Marchand playing for Team Canada, and MacKinnon on Team North America.

Canada defeated Team Europe 2-1 on Sept. 29, 2016 to sweep the best-of-three World Cup final. It was Marchand who netted the winner for Canada, scoring a short-handed goal with 44 seconds left in regulation time.

Marchand played on a line with Crosby and Patrice Bergeron at the eight-team tournament. The trio combined for 25 points and Crosby was named tournament MVP.

"Having him on your team is going to be so much more enjoyable than having to play against him," Crosby told reporters of Marchand before the World Cup began.

"Having a local guy, someone who's from the same area, I think that's pretty special to be competing for Team Canada with someone like that."

Photo by Tim Foster (@timberfoster) on Unsplash

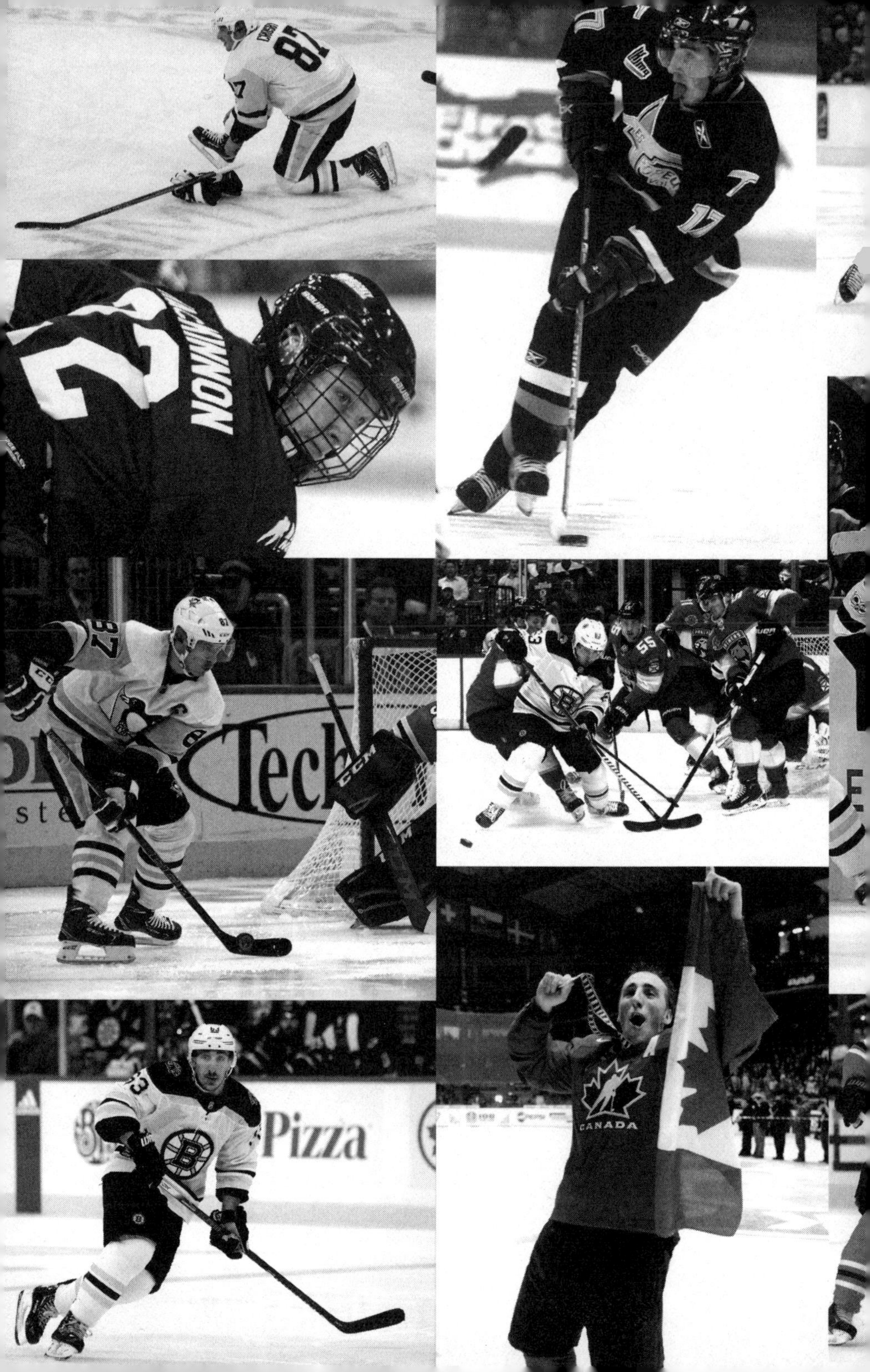
CCM
Tech
Pizza
CANADA

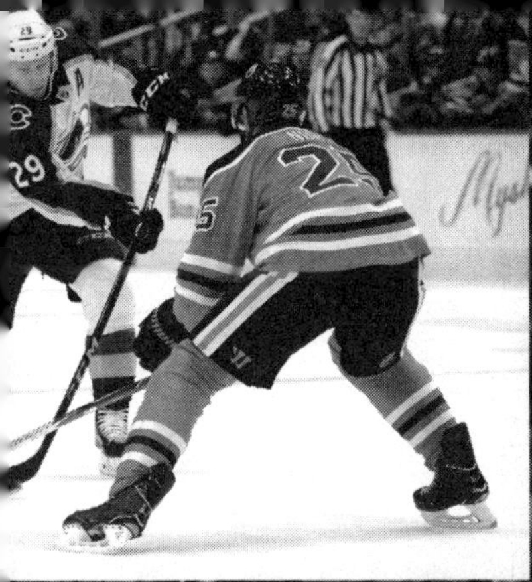

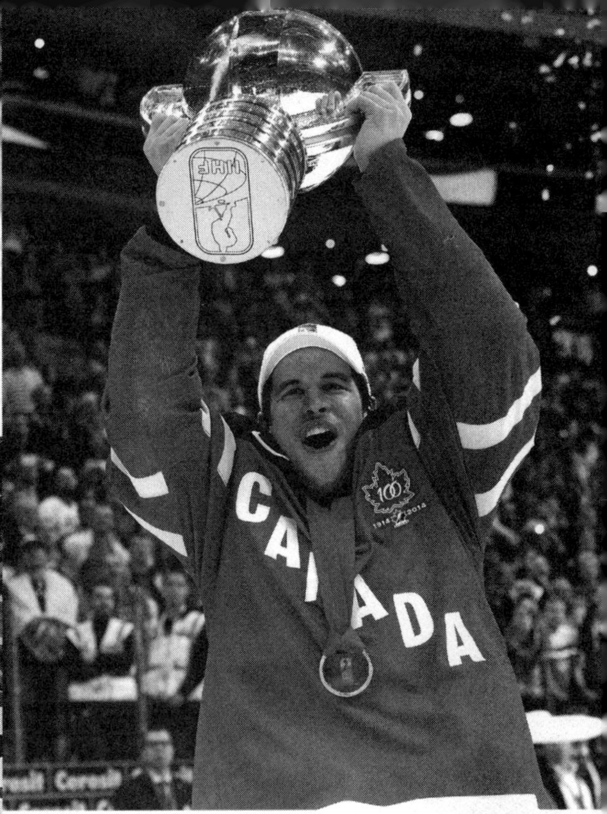

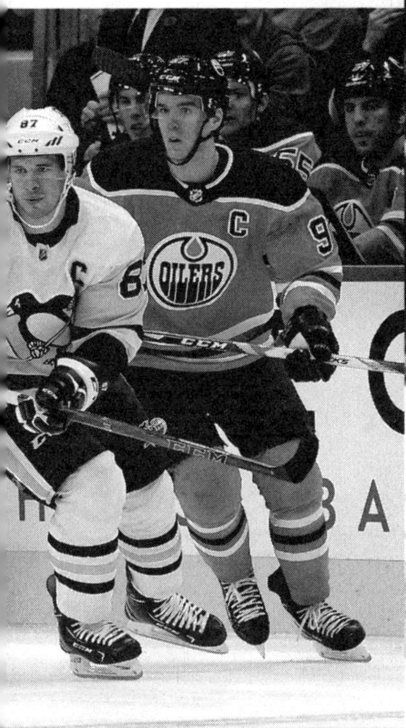
OILERS

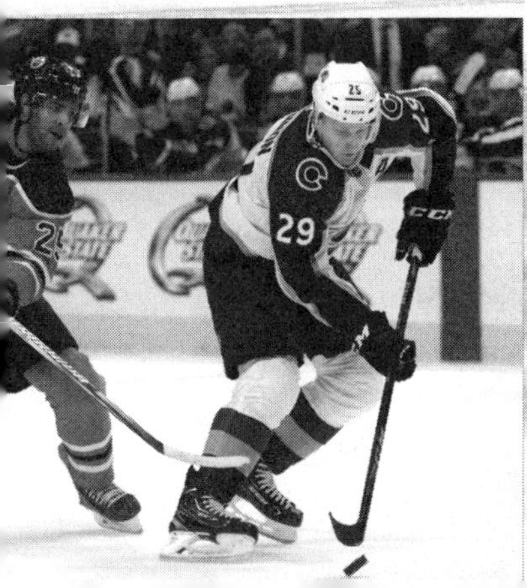

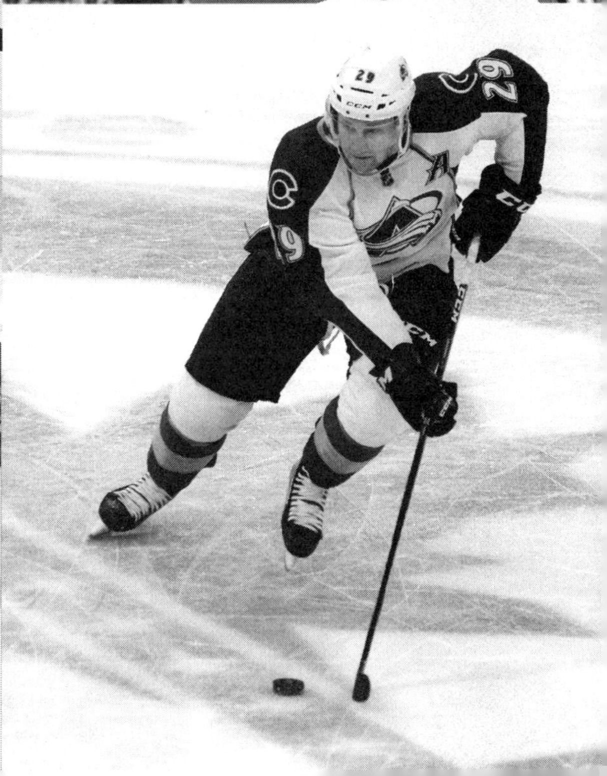